THE SPIRITUAL CONNECTION:

VALUES, FAITH, AND PSYCHOTHERAPY

by
Benjamin B. Conley

Integration of spirituality and psychotherapy based on the values and faith assumptions underlying all forms of psychotherapy.

ANTHOS Publishing
Fort Lauderdale, Florida

THE SPIRITUAL CONNECTION:
VALUES, FAITH, AND PSYCHOTHERAPY

Integration of spirituality and psychotherapy based on the values and faith assumptions underlying all forms of psychotherapy.

By Benjamin B. Conley

First Edition, 2001

Library of Congress Card Number: 2001086672

Conley, Benjamin B.
THE SPIRITUAL CONNECTION: Values, Faith, and Psychotherapy
Bibliography
Includes index.
1. Psychotherapy and spirituality. I. Title
2. Psychotherapy
3. Psychology
4. Maturation (Psychology)

ISBN 0-9708221-4-6 Pbk.

PUBLISHED BY:

ANTHOS Publishing

PO Box 4304, Fort Lauderdale, Florida 33338-4304

Dedicated to

RENA,

the person inside.

CONTENTS

CONTENTS (Continued)

CONTENTS (Continued)

CONTENTS (Continued)

CONTENTS (Continued)

FOREWARD

The author of this book has an appreciation for both scientific and spiritual worlds as these bear on an understanding of humanness and the processes of change. He has read widely and well concerning the relationship between values, faith, spirituality, and accountability/responsibility.

The insights from these readings are seasoned by the wisdom that comes from his thirty six years of therapeutic pastoral clinical teaching and practice. He formulates and presents subtle and sophisticated ideas in a very readable style. He has thought these matters through in more detail and with more care than any other author. A reader will not be left wondering, "What does he mean?"

Conley examines the basic assumptions by which we live. He spells out the impact of examining those assumptions in a therapeutic relationship. He brings a subtle and penetrating perceptivity to the discussion, keeping in mind the whole as well as the parts in his presentation. His comments on the relationship between values and spirituality break new ground, as do his thoughts on psychotherapy and faith. He illuminates the links between values and faith on the one hand, and therapeutic method on the other, as he turns theory into practice.

In an era when mental health professionals, among others, are becoming aware of the necessity for a re-examination of the topic of spirituality and values, this book will be of great interest to all who seek to be both informed and reflective with regard to the fundamentals of psychotherapy, healing, and spirituality, that is, growth in the context of wholeness.

The actual or potential client, the student-in-training, the professional therapist, the practical theologian, the clinical supervisor, the teacher; each will be interested in the material presented in this book. The book should be required reading in all programs of counselor training, regardless of profession or specialization.

This material is most timely. We are experiencing a period of history characterized by a re-thinking of context. The shift in cosmologies brought about by technology has raised the question of value premises (basic assumptions) with considerable force. Coping with this new context entails consciousness raising and reflective thought concerning globalization, inter-cultural and techno-logical communication, that is, cultural as well as individual values.

This post-modern era involves a re-thinking of economic, political, philosophical, ethical, and religious ideas and practices. The individual values that provide a basis for identity are fundamental to such an enterprise. Yet such values are not well understood.

The author makes sense of the topic, and guides the reader in doing so. He is able to relate values to both healing and spirituality in a framework that draws upon recent insights into the nature of physical and social, as well as interpersonal reality. This is no superficial treatment. Yet the reader is able to follow and master the argument so that awareness and understanding are enhanced. Hence, application becomes quite feasible.

The thesis of the following material is that, "...the communication of our positive values provides the healing power of the psychotherapeutic process." (p. 38). The task to which we are invited is to identify our most fundamental values, and the ways in which those values (and value premises) are reflected in both the theory and the technique of psychotherapy. And, "the further thesis of the book is that the functional application of positive values creates a spiritual as well as emotional connection with others, with the world in which we live, and with a life-force in the universe which is the ultimate source of healing power." (p.39).

This reader awaits with eagerness the expansion of the material presented herein to the context of the intercultural and cross-cultural counseling enterprise. While Benjamin Conley has, in my view, made a coherent and persuasive case for the central role of values in psychotherapy, he has done so in a single-culture setting. The task that awaits is one of transposing to other cultural settings the approach that is set forth with such competence here.

The Rev. John K Hinkle, Ph.D.
Professor, Pastoral Psychology and Counseling
Garrett-Evangelical Theological Seminary
Evanston, Illinois

PREFACE AND ACKNOWLEDGMENTS

All my life I have been curious about how things work, about why things are the way they are. I have admired inventors, like Thomas Edison, who experimented endlessly with one alternative after another to find a solution to a problem.

My journey of learning, I suspect like many others, has an autobiographical bias. Little did I suspect I would eventually work as a psychotherapist as I listened intently to the problems of my girlfriends in high school. Little did I understand that my interest in healing their hurts was in part to ease my own discomfort.

So I continued to learn about myself and others, and eventually began to write down what I understood about people and their functioning. This book is a kind of summary that has evolved over the past few years. I hope it can be a significant part of a mutually stimulating dialogue about the important issues of life.

The seed for this book was a course on integration of therapeutic methods I taught to other psychotherapists in the training program of the Samaritan Center of South Florida. I kept expanding on the originial lectures for the course until they reached the form you see here.

When I think of how I have been able to learn about people and relationships, I find myself deeply indebted to all those who have gone before me, studying and writing about human experience and the meaning of life. I find, upon looking back, that without being aware of it at the time, I have been building on what others have already established.

Furthermore, I find that what I experience as new is only new to me, and has been known to others for a long time. So I think my creativity consists only of putting familiar pieces together in a way not quite like anyone else has done.

For the ideas and experiences that have given me the opportunity to create, I thank all those from whom I have learned, especially friends and family from whom I have received more than I have given.

In relation to this book, I am grateful to my graduate professors, especially Nils Ehrenstrom, who believed in me, Frank West, who pursued me, Elizabeth Ehling, my first pastoral supervisor, who modeled gentleness, Smiley Blanton, my first psychiatric supervisor, who marched to his own drummer, and Yves Kron, who was patient with me and taught me much. I am indebted to hundreds of others from whom I have learned, like Michael Basch and others quoted in this book.

My colleagues have given me helpful feedback that I have incorporated into the text, and my clients have made it possible for me to have the opportunity to learn.

My students provided a stimulus to write and the D. Min. faculty at Garrett-Evangelical Theological Seminary encouraged me in developing the dimension of spirituality in the book. Other colleagues in the American Association of Pastoral Counselors have in myriad ways encouraged me to complete the book.

Rena, my wife, has been my personal consultant in the process of birthing and refining the book, reading it over and over and giving me extremely helpful commentary. She endorsed my putting so much energy into writing because she knew it to be important to me.

And I am grateful to God for the opportunity to participate in creation.

Benjamin B. Conley
Ft. Lauderdale, Florida
October, 2001

THE SPIRITUAL CONNECTION:

VALUES,
FAITH,
AND PSYCHOTHERAPY

An integration of spirituality and psychotherapy based on the values and faith assumptions underlying all forms of psychotherapy

The Search for truth is in one way hard
and in another way easy,
for it is evident that no one can master it fully
or miss it wholly.
But each adds a little to our knowledge of nature,
and from all the facts assembled
there arises a certain grandeur.

— Aristotle

INTRODUCTION

When I see clients in my office, they tell me about their pain, where the hurts in their lives occur. In doing so, they reveal the values by which they live.

Fighting, distance, and depression

One couple, troubled by their physical fights, came in for help because the wife was threatening to leave the marriage. Her husband commented casually on his knocking his wife around. "I only gave Carol a couple of smacks," he said. He grew up in a family where physical force was an ordinary way to manage relationships.

Or consider Albert, an emotionally distant person who said, out of his passivity and fear of not being perfect, "I never initiate sex with a woman. I don't want her to get the wrong idea about me, as if, you know, men are only interested in one thing." He was afraid of being rejected before he did anything.

Another man came for therapy as a last resort because he was depressed and saw his future as bleak.

He had withdrawn from his wife, his family, his professional career, and found himself isolated from others, doing a menial job to pay bills. His only friends were those he had contact with at his workplace, since he was ashamed to let his old friends know of his "failures." His mother, father, and extended family could not figure out what had happened to him, and he was too guilty about his lack of caring for his family to communicate with them.

Values and psychotherapy

These are situations familiar to psychotherapists. This book is written for all those interested in exploring how and why psychotherapy is an effective process for accomplishing positive psychological change.

One issue is of primary concern here: the commonality of values held by effective therapists, and the way those values affect the clients with whom they work. Values about life, relationships, and human nature are one of the major elements that give psychotherapy its effectiveness. As used here, values reflect our conscious and unconscious cognitive functioning, our assigning meaning to internal and external events and relationships with others.

When a change in values induces positive change, the change is expressed through a change in thinking and feeling, and also in new behavior. The way people talk to and treat each other, the way they "connect" to each other, also reflects a spiritual dimension in their relationships, open to change and growth.

PHYSICAL, EMOTIONAL, COGNITIVE, AND SPIRITUAL DIMENSIONS

The way people function is holistic and multidimensional. Each of the clients mentioned above, and others, have problems that are multi-dimensional, with all the dimensions being part of an integrated system that makes up the whole person. Looking through four dimensional "windows" may help in understanding a person's pain so as to help alleviate it. The four dimensions evolve throughout a person's life, so that they have different content and meaning as an individual goes through his or her life cycle.

The Physiological Dimension

One of the dimensions is the physiological, the biological functions that allow us to grow to adulthood and replenish cells as we go through life. Our physical functioning directly affects all the other dimensions, and might be thought of as having its primary control center in the brain stem. In addition, all the genetic information about our entire body is imbedded in the chromosomal information in every cell.

The Feeling Dimension

We experience the energy of feelings in the second, emotional dimension of life, giving us power to respond to the inner and outer stimuli of life, to invest emotional energy in what we consider important. This idea leads to other dimensions of functioning, especially our thinking and behavioral (physical) dimensions. Researchers have located the operation of feelings in the middle brain, a control center for emotions, separate from thinking.

The Cognitive Dimension

The third, cognitive dimension is intimately related to the emotional, since the way we interpret reality evokes feelings and leads to behavior that seems intuitively or logically appropriate. Learning takes place throughout our physical development, beginning as infants, before we can use the symbolic communication of language. For adults, the cerebral cortex is recognized as the general focus for operation of left and right brain types of logical and intuitive thinking.

Much of this book is written about our cognitive beliefs (even though they may be pre-verbal in origin or operation) and the way they affect our emotional responses and our behavior. We pay less attention to the reciprocal effect of behavior upon feeling and thinking, except in clinical illustrations. Overall, since we live and grow in relationships, the fourth, spiritual dimension, is inevitably part of the whole process. The resulting relative inattention to the physical dimension, and the way it affects the other dimensions does not mean we consider it unimportant, but is an arbitrary limit to the scope of the book.

The Spiritual Dimension

The spiritual dimension provides contact with all of reality as we experience it. It is understood here as our psychic "connectedness" with all that is. It is noteworthy that the Greek word *psyche,* when literally translated, means "soul." The rest of the word, psycho*logy,* coming from the Greek root, *logos,* translates into "the study of." Thus, using this logic, psychology means "the study of the soul." Psycho*therapy* would be "treatment of the soul," for the purpose of healing. This integration of spirituality and psychotherapy at least recognizes that we honor all aspects of the whole organism. At most, it means there is no psychotherapy without spirituality.

Study of the Mind and the Soul

In college psychology classes, we were first taught that psychology is the study of the mind. Years later, our teachers said the work of psychology was the study of human behavior. These two could be combined to include the study of human emotions, as well. The field has evolved and will continue to evolve with new understanding.

The view expressed here is that the inventor of the word "psychology" was intuitively closer to the mark than were his or her later teachers, and that psychology has always been the study of the soul. Psychology is thus a study of human spirituality, the way we connect to each other, to other living things, and to an energy in the universe that orders all that exists.

As a paradigm of our spiritual connections, we can note that we are all constantly and invisibly in touch with (bombarded by) television signals, radio waves, X-rays and other invisible signals. Similarly, we are invisibly in touch with human beings and other living and non-living things around us.

The Invisibility of Power

A familiar example of the existence of invisible power is the use of electricity to create light through light bulbs. With two lamps lit in the same room, we know the light produced by each lamp mixes with the light produced by the other, making an even glow throughout the room. Yet the light from each lamp is distinct from the light of the other, though we cannot distinguish the light of one from the light of the other. But when one lamp is turned off, it is clear to the eye that half the light has left the room. In this instance the light energy of one lamp has merged with the light energy of the other, all the while remaining separated.

In a similar way, the spiritual dimension and its "energy" can be thought of as part and parcel of the cognitive dimension and its "energy," which is part and parcel of the emotional dimension and its "energy," which is part and parcel of the physical dimension and its "energy," which is part and parcel of all the others, and so on in organic fashion. In each dimension, the character of the energy is different, an idea made more understandable through a comparison of the familiar differences between electro-magnetic, light, heat, and gravitational energy.

The Connectedness of All Energy

Spiritual energy is intimately connected to the physical energy created through breathing, through bringing oxygen to the lungs and thence to the blood. Blood in turn takes nourishment and renewal to the entire body. In some religious traditions, God breathed life into persons as part of the creation of life. Perhaps the inner energy related to breathing and the body's use of oxygen is partly why one's body and self-image is so closely connected with his or her name and identity.

The Use of Energy for Good or Ill

How we use our spiritual energy to connect to others is reflected in our feeling and thinking, and especially in our behavior. The behavior of human beings spans a wide range. We know of saintly persons who demonstrate emotional caring for others, like Albert

Schweitzer, who spent his life as a doctor expressing his love and respect for all living things. His countryman, Adolf Hitler, spent his life expressing and acting on his hatred and contempt for others. What is the common human nature that binds us all together? The spiritual dimension can apparently be used for evil as well as for good, an expression of our values and the relative wellness of our psyche/soul.

Our Limited Understanding of Reality

Human nature has been spoken and written about for centuries. It is an inextricable mixture of philosophy, theology, politics, war, economics, dramatic arts, and so on. Many writers have made profound comments on and written books about various aspects of the nature of man. But no general consensus about the nature of human nature has emerged. Maybe we can learn from this lack of consensus over the past 4,000 years and conclude that people each have their own ways of seeing reality, including the reality of human nature, not quite like others see it.

The Five Blind Men

Here is a classic example. Several blind men had a communication difficulty as they examined an elephant. One found it to be like a leaf (the ear), another like a rope (the tail), another like a snake (the trunk), another like a tree (the leg), and another like a wall (the side). They argued with each other, each certain he had the correct understanding. But they were all correct, demonstrating that "both, and" is a more useful hypothesis than "either, or." Various points of view each can have some validity, even when they are very different from each other.

Perhaps we can come to the conclusion that each person's point of view has been shaped by an idiosyncratic set of historical events, and that the autobiographical flavor of any theory on the nature of human nature requires that the theory be seen as limited, partial, distorted, and biased. (Von Glaserfeld discusses these limitations in his book, *The Invented Reality.*) Inevitably, we can only function from within our own frame of reference, based on our own experience and knowledge of the world.

Historical experience is not the only influence on our view of things. The way our bodies process data also makes a difference. S. I. Hayakawa, in *Language in Thought and Action,* pp. 176-177, writes, "The way in which we happen to see and feel things is the result of the peculiarities of our nervous systems. There are 'sights' we cannot see, and, as even children know today with their high frequency dog whistles, 'sounds' that we cannot hear." He suggests that it is absurd, therefore, to imagine that we ever perceive anything as it really is.

Our Search for Truth

However we perceive it, most will agree that it is desirable to understand the nature of man "as it is," but there is much disagreement on just what that nature is. This disagreement provides a perspective from which we can acknowledge the limitations and inadequacy of any particular theory of the nature of human nature, including anything written here.

How then, can we write anything about the nature of human nature? One answer is that we can write about what we currently understand, with the knowledge that we can modify our understanding based on new information. As time goes by, we have additional experience on which to come to new conclusions.

For example, the work of Stephen Hawking on "Black Holes" in the universe established the previously unthinkable fact that some stars may contract to such a degree that their light is no longer visible. These stars become invisible since their light no longer expands outward. At the same time they betray their existence by still exerting a gravitational force that can be measured. These invisible-to-the-eye stars are "visible" to gravitational detection and are called black holes.

Learning from experience as we go is probably the best we can do, even though this solution means we must deal with our reluctance to re-examine fundamental assumptions, once adopted, including the ones presented here. Old habits are difficult to change, even when the new habits will be to our advantage.

THE STRENGTH OF FUNDAMENTAL VALUES

Sam, over a number of years, earned the reputation, "he is as honest at the day is long." This made him trustworthy in the eyes of others, even though he did not have to think about being honest. "That's just the way I am," he said. He could be trusted to keep his word, to honor his obligations, and to treat others fairly.

Consistency of Personality Structure

The ability we all have to proceed "on automatic" without constantly re-examining the principles upon which we base our lives is a great strength. Otherwise, we would be paralyzed by constantly re-evaluating our values and the methods used to express them. Instead, we establish our values with long term consistency and know how we will apply them with a set of behaviors that others recognize as part of our personality style.

This strength, based on consistency, may sometimes create a difficulty, since its purpose is to resist fundamental change. Imagine that Sam is *dis*honest instead of honest, and that he wishes to change to become "honest." He may have difficulty making the change. Such a change in a "foundation" value requires him to reconstruct his entire system. In order to move the foundation, the entire house has to be dismantled and rebuilt in a new way. When we wish to make fundamental changes in our values, we will find it difficult to modify our established life structures.

The Effect of Values on Behavior

For example, in the United States we have learned over the past fifty years that sexual and physical child abuse is destructive and therefore unacceptable. Yet, at one time, the adage, "Spare the rod and spoil the child" was almost universally accepted as true, and no one wanted a "spoiled" child. As a culture, we are learning that it is not necessary to physically attack children in order to teach them how to live as socially productive persons. Such an approach is based on fear. There are better ways to accomplish this goal, but the integration into culture of better ways is difficult and time consuming.

Perhaps a resolution of this dilemma of resistance to change is to redefine the meaning of change. We can think of change as inherently desirable, ***provided it enhances previously defined fundamental values that are not up for change.*** If we attempt to change what is most fundamentally positive about ourselves, we risk redefining ourselves out of existence and into another meaning of "human."

As an illustration in the physical arena, if we were to decide people should not have legs, we would be proposing a value -- no legs -- that would result in people being fundamentally different. If we were to put that value into effect, the difference would be so great that people would not be human beings, and we would have to invent another name for them. We would have changed the meaning of "human nature."

In the psychological arena, a fundamental value is that tools are useful in solving problems. If we were to negate this value, we would be recommending that people function at such a primitive level that they would no longer be using their cerebral cortex to solve problems, a redefinition of human nature.

Another example is the social value of our commitment to freedom of speech and action. This value is supported so long as our speech and action is not designed to destroy the right to freedom of speech and action. Freedom is so basic to human nature that some have dramatically said, as Patrick Henry did, "Give me liberty or give me death," defining freedom as such an important value that he would die defending it. The mottos of several states reflect a similar commitment.

An example in a religious context is our belief in the fundamental value of love as a desirable basis for relating to others, shared by so many of the world religions. One expression of love is the commitment that each religious group is free to worship differently, ruling out any thought or attempt to limit the freedom of others to worship in their own way.

Fundamental Values as Essential

A primary value endorsed here is that change and growth are desirable, so long as the change does not destroy our fundamental values. Instead, positive change endorses and protects our fundamental values. Just as we know bones in our body are fundamental to adequate human physical functioning, there are "bones" essential to our psychological, emotional, and spiritual functioning as well. The fundamentals provide structure upon which to build our lives, just as bones provide the structure needed for physical functioning. This book outlines and describes some of those fundamental structures - values - in an attempt to clarify them and stimulate thinking about them.

Ultimately, the foundations of physical, emotional, and cognitive functioning are aspects of one entire interacting system that has a dimension of spiritual "connectedness," the parts being focused upon separately only for purposes of discussion. The connection we make with others, based on our commitment to common values, and the way we express them in our behavior are parts of the spiritual dimension of life.

HUMAN NATURE AND THE NATURE OF KNOWLEDGE

Thinking about human nature leads to thinking about the nature of knowledge. One can raise the question, "What can we know about human nature for sure?" and "How do we know what we know?" These are subjects that have entranced seminal thinkers for centuries.

A Philosophical Issue

One of the first philosophers to create a coherent theory of knowledge was Plato. "He agreed with Socrates that sense perception could not give genuine knowledge. Man must pass beyond the senses to ideas which are not derived from experience and are not dependent upon experience." (S. E. Frost, Jr., *Ideas of the Great Philosophers,* p. 280). This quotation raises many questions, including that of how one can escape being bound by the limitations of his or her own experience.

Another thinker, Aristotle, committed to knowing the reasons for things, worked out the rules for formal logic, which remain the same today. He made a major contribution to our understanding of the way logical thinking "works," establishing tools to differentiate clear from muddled or illogical reasoning, a help in identifying what is true or false.

Other philosophers, like Descartes, Kant, Hegel, and Dewey, have contributed to understanding the nature of knowledge, evolving toward the idea by the 1950's that "ideas are tools for solving problems. Thinking is a way one may go about meeting difficult situations. . . . If, by thinking, he solves his problem, the process has been satisfactory and his ideas true." (*Ideas of the Great Philosophers,* p. 294).

Your Understanding of Human Nature

No doubt, the reader could also contribute to the dialogue about the nature of knowledge, a dialogue that will go on as long as people have ideas about thinking and knowledge. The objective here is not to summarize our knowledge about human nature. Nor is the objective here to *settle* issues about how psychotherapy affects human functioning in a positive way. Rather, it is to suggest a framework within which we may identify and think about the values underlying the practice of psychotherapy as an essential part of the healing process.

WE KNOW ONLY WHAT WE KNOW

For the purpose of thinking about what we know about psychotherapy, a pragmatic approach may be useful, without begging other theoretical questions. A way to state that approach is that *"we do well to know what we know, to know what we do not know, and to be clear about the difference."* This principle, knowing what we know, what we don't know, and the difference between the two, can be used for practical guidance.

We can be clear within ourselves what we are certain of, acknowledging our uncertainties, and not mixing the two. We can reserve the right to modify any idea. But in the meantime, we know what we know and know what we're unsure of. The next question becomes "How do we know what we know?"

Facts as Based on Consensus

Instead of wading into this wasp's nest of issues, let us settle for another pragmatic principle. We can think of "facts" as being ideas that are currently accepted by our professional colleagues, subject to continuing challenge and clarification. This might seem to be another wasp's nest, since large areas of disagreement may exist, leaving areas where we don't know the "facts." Yet, it is the process of collegial scientific validation, by which we may eventually arrive at a consensus.

For example, most of our professional colleagues would probably agree with Piaget's findings about experiential learning in infants. Agreement in this context probably means acknowledgment that his contributions have been significant and that they have greatly influenced our understanding of child development. One of his findings is summarized in his book on *Structuralism* on page 63, where he relates his understanding of structural elements to what he calls the functional factors of *assimilation* and *accommodation.*

As another example, most of our professional colleagues would probably agree about the importance of "systems" in affecting the individual's relationships with others. Napier and Whitaker describe a view of systems in family therapy (*The Family Crucible*, p. 49), in a way that expresses a fairly common point of view:

> "This is an interesting characteristic of living systems. . . . they make changes in their own behavior based on information about their environment. This mechanism, called feedback, permits the system to alter its activity, its structure, its direction, in order to further its own goals. . . The comparison may seem strained, but the systems concept allows one to compare the simple organism like the amoeba with the more complex system like the family."

What We Know, Don't Know, and the Difference Between Them

We can agree on what we "know" to be true, what we accept as valid for now, and whether we have agreement with others.

We can also identify what we "don't know," the part about which we are ignorant or uncertain.

We can also be clear about *the difference* between what we "know" and "don't know." Most of what we all accept and agree upon can be qualified and hedged in some way, making us aware of a continuum from certainty to the totally unknown.

There is a further distinction to be made between what we know and what we don't know. That difference is characterized by ambiguity. We know what we know, except that even our knowledge (what we "know") is subject to revision, and we don't know which ideas will eventually be modified. Not knowing what will change is part of what we "don't know." This ambiguity about the ultimate validity of "facts" is what allows us to keep our knowledge and communication about human nature open-ended, not written in stone.

The Limits to Consensus

The further we extend the concentric circles in our professional community, the less agreement we will find. For example, if we were to take a poll of a group of psychologists, they might agree on a set of facts learned in graduate school, and agree to a lesser degree on additional facts learned from later training to be psychotherapists. Even so, their accumulation of knowledge might be similar enough to the knowledge shared by other groups of psychologists to allow all to pass the appropriate state and national licensing exams.

However, when the circle of professional colleagues is expanded to include social workers, the chance of consensus is reduced. When psychiatrists are included, still less commonality is found. When licensed psychotherapists from other disciplines are added, consensus is still more difficult. A national licensing board would find it a strenuous task to write exam questions satisfactory to all the professional groups mentioned.

WE CAN AGREE ON FUNDAMENTALS

We may find a high degree of agreement *on fundamentals* by psychotherapists from all disciplines. As an example of agreement on the fundamentals in the physical dimension, we can note the near universal acceptance of Gray's *Anatomy* as a classic description of human anatomy, still used as a text in medical schools.

Or, as other examples, most people might agree that they see a wheel as round at the circumference. Most will agree it is easier to see in the daytime than at night. Health care workers might agree that the brain continues to develop along with the rest of the body at least until puberty, when the capacity for abstract symbolic thinking is fully established. These are all biologically determined fundamentals.

Physical Touch Is Essential for Life

Another biologically determined fundamental is the need of infants to be touched and held as infants. Without touch, an infant seems to give up on living, and will eventually die, as if an inner light flickers and goes out. It is a basic matter of life and death, and is generally understood and accepted by health care workers.

The life-giving power of human contact can also be understood as a spiritual connection, not in addition to, but built into the genetic structure of life. There seems to be a life-giving force that cannot be seen or measured, but that can be identified as present when health and wholeness is also present. Candace Pert is the molecular biologist who discovered the opiate receptor on body cells. She comments in *Healing and the Mind,* that when someone dies, a "spark" seems to leave the body, something more than the cessation of cell activity.

Fundamental Assumptions: Values

In addition, other fundamentals are determined by the emotional and cognitive development of each individual. These two dimensions seem intimately related to each other, since cognitive meaning (even when non-verbal) is assigned to incoming internal and external stimulation. Emotional responses appropriate and proportional to the assigned meaning follow automatically, giving the subjective sense that we are not in direct control of our feelings.

A number of assumptions can be made about what is supportive of the human developmental process, based on studies and experience with human development. My using the words "fundamental" and "assumptions" together might seem inconsistent, since anything fundamental might be expected to be more than an assumption. However, use of the word, "assumptions," is meant to acknowledge that many of our operational principles cannot be proven by scientific study, much less double blind experiments under controlled conditions.

Further, use of the word, assumptions, implies that they may be modified, leaving our knowledge "open ended." To think of knowledge as open ended is also consistent with the historical reality that not everyone agrees, even with what I am calling "fundamental assumptions."

I think it is more realistic and honest to speak of assumptions about fundamentals, since fundamentals are so difficult to prove. For example, the question of whether a human being has inherent value can be debated endlessly from a theoretical point of view, and will never be fully resolved through scientific study.

As an example of a pragmatic operational assumption, it can be clinically demonstrated that valuing oneself and others supports emotional and physical health, while de-valuing oneself and others destroys well being. Psychotherapists would likely agree with this idea, since it is basic to the work of psychotherapy. It is also basic to the maintenance of social and political order.

However, social and political application of the principle that human life has great value has been uneven, and historically has been marked with incidents that devalue human life. The development of slavery, wherever it has existed, including the United States, expressed that devaluation. So did the liquidation of Armenians at the time of the first world war. So did the use of children as child laborers in the late 1800's and following. So did the destruction of Jews in Germany in the 1940's. And so on.

On the other hand, the examples above serve to highlight the importance of valuing human life. One illustration could be that our consensus that life is to be nurtured and not destroyed is a fundamental assumption. It is assumed and expressed in our psychotherapeutic theories and techniques.

This book is about identifying our most fundamental values, and how our value assumptions show up in both our therapeutic theories and our therapeutic techniques, our ways of treating others, what we say and do. The thesis is that the communication of our positive values provides the healing power of the psychotherapeutic process.

THE SPIRITUAL CONNECTION

The further thesis of the book is that the functional application of positive values affirms a spiritual, as well as emotional connection with others, with the world in which we live, and with a life-force in the universe which is the ultimate source of healing power.

A Positive Life-Force

This is the force that causes plants and animals to grow. It is the force that makes subatomic particles move. It is the force that moves radio waves through doors and walls.

This is the force that gives life to the "touched" child, the absence of which results in death for the "untouched" child. We all intuitively know the emotional importance of holding and cuddling a child, of loving an infant, and are familiar with spontaneously responding to a child with warmth and love. It might be argued that the infant is biologically equipped to emit just the sounds necessary to evoke our nurturing response.

Such a nurturing response nourishes a loving emotional and spiritual connection, an experience of our common humanity, tapping the power that gives life to that humanity.

Our Treatment of Each Other Counts

From this illustration, we can see that it is possible to identify *ways of treating each other* that give life (e.g. holding and nurturing), and *ways of treating each other* that are destructive (condemnation, attack, and rejection). By identifying values that form the basis of loving behavior, we define the position from which we can affirm emotional and spiritual connections with others in ways that nourish life. Equally important, we define a position from which we can participate in the life-force that is greater than ourselves, even though it is greater than we will ever fully understand.

We have the practical advantage of not having to understand everything before we act. We can identify certain values as positive enough for everyday living that we can endorse them without reservation. And we have the added practical advantage of not having to understand how spirituality "works" before participating in it. We already participate in a spiritual connection with others when we "join" with them in the therapeutic process.

Spirituality Reflects Connectedness

We learn by experience what being spiritually connected means at various stages of our lives, as we accept and affirm our connection to others. We can be connected in deeply personal ways, like the connection to our birth mother, or in very limited ways, like the connection to the newly acquired pet fish won at a game at the state fair.

We can be cognitively aware of the connection and how it defines the meaning of the realtionship to us. The connection is also emotional, related to our affective responses, and it is spiritual, related to our participation in that which supports life for all of us. By choosing to be intentional about participating in the process of spiritual involvement, we can enhance and support the growth process, in ourselves and in others.

Because our biological, emotional, cognitive, and social growth is developmentally formed, our spiritual connections and experiences are developmentally defined. That is, the way we connect emotionally and spiritually with an infant is different from the way we connect emotionally and spiritually with a teenager.

The spiritual connection is important in every part of our developmental journey, from birth to old age, if health is to be maintained at the optimum. Put negatively, isolation and rejection is painful and destructive of well-being, wherever we are in life's journey.

Our Spiritual Connection is Invisible

We cannot describe and define our spiritual connection with others *directly and concretely,* since the connection is non-cognitive and non-specific in nature. However, we can identify the values we hold, which, when acted upon, result in the creation of a positive spiritual connection (or a negative spiritual connection, if the values are destructive). The content of spirituality is a co-creation with another or others, and can never be seen, though the results may be evident to observers.

Based on what has been said above, the over-arching framework of this book is that all forms of psychotherapy are based on underlying values and faith assumptions. These values open the door to the cognitive, emotional, and spiritual connections that allow us to participate most fully in the healing process, for others and for ourselves.

CHAPTER I
THREE PSYCHOLOGICAL FUNDAMENTALS

Natalie's story is a success story. She used psychotherapy to reorganize her life from top to bottom, reviewing and modifying learnings developed in her first thirty years of life. When she first came to therapy she was having difficulty with her marriage.

The Struggle to Become Lovable

First she grappled with her anger, pain, and fear at having been reared by a mother who was so emotionally hungry that she did not have much love to give her children. Instead, her mother was preoccupied with what Natalie and her brother would do for her.

Naturally her mother was also very angry, since small children need more than they can give, while her mother wanted it the other way around. So Natalie learned she was not wanted and was a "bother," not worth much to her mother at all.

Her Discovery That She Was Always Lovable

Natalie's belief that she was not lovable was the first therapeutic issue with which to deal. She learned that her mother's lack of interest in her, her harsh criticisms, and sending her to boarding school did *not* mean she was worthless as a person, but *did* mean her mother didn't know how to love her unconditionally.

Her mother was preoccupied with her own internal pain and depression. Natalie learned that her mother's treatment of her told much about her mother and very little about herself. Natalie grieved a great deal over not having received unconditional love from her mother.

Most important, Natalie learned that she is worthy of being loved, that her mother's inability to be nurturing was not caused by her, but was her mother's limitation.

She also learned that not everyone is as limited as her mother was, that others have the capacity for nurturing, affection, and empathy.

This new understanding, arrived at with much struggle and pain, created a new certainty that she was important just because she existed as an individual person, the first psychological fundamental assumption about which we are writing.

Natalie's father was no help because he was not there -- distant, uninvolved in the family, spending most of his time at his job. He and his wife did not know how to love and be close to each other, and they were divorced by the time Natalie was ten years old.

When she was twenty two she married a man she hoped would take care of her in ways her parents did not. She took several years to accept that her husband would not respond to her attempts to have a loving relationship, and they were finally divorced when she was thirty three.

The Struggle to Become Independent

As Natalie grieved about the lack of early nurturing from her mother and father, she began to face her anger at the manipulative and domineering qualities of her mother, which she also found in her husband, Frank, and to some degree in herself.

Natalie had lived her life up to this time attempting to control others by using the same methods her mother had used to manipulate those around her. By trying to control others' reactions and behavior she helped maintain some order in her life, some constancy.

But, since people cannot be controlled by others, Natalie lived in a constant state of anxiety, lest others do the unplanned and unexpected. This high anxiety was another reason she originally came into therapy.

The Discovery She Does Control Herself

She had great difficulty reversing her field and integrating the belief that she couldn't control others' thinking, feeling, and behavior. As she gradually became more comfortable with that reality, she gave up her goal of controlling others. She claimed, instead, the ability to make her own decisions and control herself. She found that she had been making her own decisions, even when she chose to "give herself away" to others.

She gradually accepted others' right to make their own decisions for themselves, even when they were different than decisions she would have made.

This process affected and changed every aspect of her life, including the way she managed herself physically. She improved her diet, made exercise a regular part of her daily routine, and gradually came to think of herself as more attractive.

Throughout the time she was integrating valuing herself into her daily routine and applying her new understanding of autonomy, she practiced relating to others without attempting to control them, learning to appreciate them, instead.

She was successful in restructuring her life on this new basis of freedom to choose, but was still subject to periods of intense anxiety for other reasons. Natalie had established the principle of independence for herself and others in most areas of her life, though she did not always approve of what she or others did, thought or felt.

She had established the principle that she and every person is entitled to make his or her own decisions, the second of the fundamental psychological assumptions described here, but she was still "in trouble" emotionally.

The Struggle to Choose Her Own Drummer

Her second long term relationship with a man did not include marriage, expressing her avoidance of "commitment" that seemed necessary at the time to keep her independence. But as she became clearer about how to be close and independent at the same time, she wanted more involvement in a relationship. She moved on to another man whom she eventually married.

She was ready for more intimacy, realizing that she could find a way to create closeness with another person who also valued separateness and independence. She terminated therapy because of her success, determined to put her knowledge to work in her marriage.

This new relationship was the occasion to deal with another set of issues: how to enjoy differences and how to negotiate disagreements.

After a time, she came back to therapy to deal with those concerns. While still integrating the first two principles into her life more fully, she focused in therapy on how to have a close realtionship while respecting the other person's differences and supporting the other's growth.

Seen subjectively, the issue was the maintenance and enhancement of her own self-esteem in contrast to her remaining apprehension that she could not "measure up" to others' expectations.

Her fear was that when people, including her husband, found out she was not perfect, she would be rejected and condemned as she was by her mother and the teachers she had tolerated in her boarding school.

The process of learning how to accept others as they are (and herself, as well) was especially difficult for Natalie, who had just been getting used to having the right to manage her own life as a separate person.

How to relate to all those other separate persons presented a dilemma because of the newness of the pattern and fear that if she did the new and different she would be rejected or attacked for behaving in a new way.

The thousands of applications of the principle that she had the right to live her life her own way and allow others the same privilege took time to integrate into her life. In effect, she taught herself what her parents did not know how to teach her, using her own resources, including the ability to arrange for a consultant, in the form of a therapist, to assist her in the process.

A Pyramid of Values

Using Natalie's story, we can view value assumptions about how to live as having three "layers," like a pyramid made of three sections, each one placed on top of the one below.

The most basic, foundation layer is composed of the three psychological fundamentals. The next layer consists of four later developmental learnings. The top, pointed layer is the fifteen other beliefs that grow out of establishing the first two layers.

This chapter is about the bottom layer, the first three psychological fundamentals, as illustrated in Natalie's therapeutic journey.

These three fundamental assumptions may be shared and affirmed by most professional psychotherapists, in terms of their current thinking. Although these three beliefs would be stated differently by different writers, they also contain a common thread of similarity.

The Foundation of the Pyramid

The first of the three fundamentals is that every human being has value, as a separate individual, simply because of his or her existence. This belief forms an operational foundation on the basis of which to live life, as well as to do therapy.

The second fundamental is that people make decisions for themselves, and manage their own behavior, thoughts, and fcelings by being in control of their own bodies. This is less a belief and more a description of the way people function, even when they choose to give away their autonomy as a way to survive by being subservient to others.

The third fundamental is that people think and act on the basis of their own best judgment, in their own way, using their own experience. We pursue what we consider to be our best options at any given time.

These most basic assumptions might be thought of as the bedrock of beliefs about people, the most basic of basics. They are the assumptions that describe what we would consider to be the psychological and emotional essentials in our approach to clients and each other.

This is why they form the foundation layer of our pyramid. We have used them as a way to understand the process of therapy with Natalie.

We assume that these three principles are so basic to human nature that they are not subject to change. They might be better stated or the implications more clearly spelled out than they are here, but they are, for purposes of this discussion, not subject to negotiation or cancellation.

When people do not agree about these three fundamentals, it is easy to understand why there may be disagreement and conflict about other, less basic matters. When conflict is caused by negation of these fundamentals, the persons doing so engage in adverserial and self-defensive behavior.

Such behavior creates much individual anguish, as well as pain and suffering in family, community, ethnic, national, and international relationships.

Let us examine these three fundamentals in more detail, even though they may seem self evident.

1a) PEOPLE HAVE VALUE BECAUSE THEY EXIST

The first psychological fundamental is that we have value unconditionally, because we exist, before we do anything, a central tenet of many religious traditions.

As one of my clients told me about the view of himself he developed as a child, he called himself "garbage." He thought his parents didn't want him, that they wished he had not been born, and so he saw himself as having no more value than a piece of trash or garbage to be discarded, except for the rules of society against throwing children away.

As a result he viewed himself as a burden that made his parents' lives miserable. His parents had not conveyed to him a sense of his great value as an individual human being. He suffered great unhappiness and had severe difficulty in creating a productive life, since he devalued himself and everything he did.

We need to be "in positive contact" with other human beings, physically and emotionally, through touching and other forms of communication. This is the foundation of affirmation of the value of one's existence.

Ultimately, each person needs to make this a self-affirmation by soaking up the affirmation offered by others, starting with one's caretakers at birth. Self-affirmation is also the foundation of a spiritual connection that flows through the physical and emotional experience of loving and being loved, validating a person's existence in the world, and providing an internal sense of "belonging."

Sometimes the most common experiences illustrate a point most clearly. For example, we have all experienced the sound of infants crying with some kind of discontent. We have also watched as they (sometimes) become magically quiet and content when picked up by the mother. The reassurance that comes from contact with the mothering person provides unconditional affirmation, essential emotional "food."

If we receive this relatively unconditional affirmation from others as an infant and small child, we may incorporate a belief in our own value essential for our emotional well being. If we do not receive this affirmation that we have value just be virtue of existing, we may find ourselves as adults complaining of "emptiness" in our lives, a sense of "part of us missing," a fear of abandonment, or a chronic "loneliness" that seems incurable.

Loneliness and a fear of abandonment was Natalie's dilemma when she came into therapy, having had a narcissistic mother with little capacity for empathy and nurturing. She tried to fill her deep loneliness with a relationship with a man and with money, to replace the love her mother couldn't give. Natalie finally gave up the struggle to get her mother to be more loving and grieved about what her mother didn't and couldn't give.

Her grieving left her open to and able to take in the affirmation of others who were different from her mother, who did have love to give. She could not convert her mother into someone more loving. She could not go back and re-live the past to make her mother love her differently. But she could be in contact with people in the present and future who have the capacity to love and to communicate with love, acceptance, and affirmation.

We Need Others According to Our Growth

We never grow out of our need to be in communication with others, to have other important people in our lives. We begin with the need to be held and loved as an infant. Even after successfully taking in unconditional affirmation from others, learning we have value just because we exist, we still need to be in touch with others who are important to us.

We need that nurturing from others as children, to help us deal with later developmental tasks. But in addition, our positive contact with others provides an essential nutrient for our emotional functioning.

This continuing need for contact is not only for the purpose of reassuring ourselves about our value. It is for the purpose of sharing what we consider to be of value in our own lives and hearing about the same from others, a process of mutual enrichment and nurturing. Such sharing with others provides the psychological and emotional basis for personal security and for living in community with other people. It represents our spiritual connection with others.

Sharing Opens the Way to Spirituality

Sharing with others validates a spiritual connection with them. This connection begins with conception and the intimate relationship with the mother *in utero* and continues with her and others the rest of one's life. We can affirm this spiritual connectedness even though we cannot quantify and define it.

Spirituality is more than our emotional response to what others do or say. Spirituality has to do with the human connection we make to others in the process of our thinking, feeling, and actions, the connection of one's inner self with the inner self of the other.

In a totally precognitive way, the infant experiences the spiritual connection through affirmation of his or her value. Later, the toddler experiences it as affirmation of his or her autonomy. It is what the older child experiences as affirmation of his or her creativity. The spiritual dimension is inevitably present in the way we relate to others at every emotional developmental level.

1b) INDIVIDUALS ARE SEPARATE FROM EACH OTHER

This first fundamental has a second part. The first part, already discussed above, is the need to be valued without having to “earn” that love. The second part is the need to be valued *as an individual person,* separate from parents and others. I will illustrate this principle of separation with the following example.

Rayna first came to my office because of difficulty with her in-laws. There had been no problem for the first six years of marriage, because her husband had no significant relationship with his mother and father, and had established his own life on his own terms. After the arrival of a child two years earlier, he made contact with his parents and extended family (brothers, sisters, and their spouses and children), and they began to visit on holidays.

The problem Rayna faced was the openly stated demand by her inlaws that she should join with their position that "women are inferior to men," that she should cater to the wishes of her mother-in-law, that those who differ from them should be rejected, and that, in general, in any relationship, one person is to be dominant and the other submissive. They quoted the Bible as "The husband is head of the wife."

This disallowance of differences between her and her in-laws was unfamiliar to Rayna, and at the time of our first session, she was confused and wondered if she were wrong. She wondered whether she had the right to object to being told she should change her ways and do as she was told by her in-laws. She gradually began to realize that they were operating within a system that did not allow for individual differences and the right of each person to enjoy being separate from others.

The Process of Differentiation

The process of differentiation begins early in infancy as a child first learns to tell one face from another, to know a parent from a stranger. It continues with the brain development that, for example, later allows the discovery that covering a toy with a cloth doesn't make it disappear.

By seven or eight months of age, a child will make a dramatic discovery: that when the mother leaves the room or the house, she really "goes away" and is not still around to be called back at will. The mother has *really* left the child, though another caretaker may be there to care for his or her needs.

This realization is sometimes upsetting to the child, but is part of learning that being separate is inevitable, and not really a disaster. The mother does eventually return.

As we each learn to differentiate ourselves from others, we discover that whatever exists outside our own skin is "not me." We live only within our own body.

Application of this principle means that each person crawls, walks, talks, and feels separately from others. When successful in learning to value our separateness, we learn to enjoy it and to develop a clear sense of the boundaries between ourselves and others.

The physical manifestation of this separation is our skin, defining our "self" as what is physically inside our skin. Our self, emotionally and psychologically, is an extension of this physical reality. Relating to others then becomes something we do as separate persons, rather than being connected in an undifferentiated manner.

This is an area in which Natalie, the woman described earlier in this chapter, had less difficulty. Being very intelligent and left to her own devices much of the time, she was on her own very early in life. She accepted her separateness from her mother as a way to be liberated from the emotional demands of her mother.

Since her mother did as little as possible for her, she experienced her mother as uninterested, someone to protect herself from, not to be dependent upon. Ironically, in the midst of her dependence on others, including housekeepers, she learned that depending on one person for everything was not the most successful way to get her needs met.

The Solution to Co-Dependence

Clarity about being separate is the antidote to "co-dependence," in which the boundaries between people are not clear, and we mistakenly take responsibility for others' thinking, feeling, and behavior, as if we were in charge of those processes in the other person, as if we were living within the other person's body.

One life, our own, is all each person has to manage, and is indeed enough to manage, since we live in our own body, not in anyone else's body.

We do well, however, to take responsibility for managing others to the degree they are incompetent to do so for themselves. The most obvious instance is our caring for children, who cannot totally care for themselves. In the normal course of adult living, however, each person is in charge of only his or her own decision-making, not the decision-making of others.

Caring Instead of Caretaking

Being responsible only for one's own decisions is a concept that is difficult for many people to understand or to accept, because it seems to them to imply no caring and no relationship at all between people.

Instead, it actually implies a particular kind of relationship between people, one that offers caring and respect for the other person's integrity as a separate person with his or her own individual ideas, emotions, and behaviors. The caring is expressed without caretaking, without taking responsibility for the other person's thinking, feeling, and behavior.

We can care about each other and respect the other person's separateness as part of that caring. We can act in a loving or friendly manner without taking over the responsibility for the management of the person we love. We can act in a loving or friendly manner even though the other person does not know what is going on within our minds or feelings.

We Are a Stimulus, Not a Cause

When we put out a stimulus to others, they will respond in some way. What we do is perceived by others through their senses: hearing, seeing, touching, smelling, or tasting. They will respond to what we say or do, but on their own terms, since being separate allows for their being different and responding uniquely.

The concept of stimulus and response presupposes separate persons, each with their own apparatus for sending signals, for receiving them, and for determining what to do in response. This separateness is the condition for having a relationship of two or more persons, since without the separation, each of us could only relate to an extension of ourselves.

2) PEOPLE MAKE DECISIONS GOVERNING THEMSELVES

The second psychological fundamental is the belief that we are in charge of our own lives, the "executive directors" of our own thinking, feeling, and acting.

As children, we all need to experience encouragement and support to exercise increasing control over our own body. This means the obvious, that we each control our talking, walking, thinking, and other bodily activities. We can crawl, stand up, lie down, run, jump up and down, talk, sing, or do many other things, depending on our choice of what to do.

When emotionally successful in this area of physical development, we establish an affirmation of our right to exercise self-control. This gives an internal psychological "structure" to our life, providing a sense of being self-directing, the opposite of being victimized by other people and events. We know we are in charge of our decision-making, our "yes" and our "no."

We Are in Control of Our Own Bodies

Learning that we are in control of our own bodies begins early in life, as we grow into the ability to crawl, walk, talk, and become more physically competent. One of the common ways a child uses to establish a sense of autonomy is to say or do the opposite of what he or she is asked to do by the caretaking adult. Oppositional behavior is one way the child gains reassurance that he or she is not being dominated by someone else.

It may seem strange that as children we may not have clearly learned we are in control of our own bodies, since it is so obvious that we are. No one else moves my arm for me, unless I agree for someone to physically do so, or unless I am physically under the control of others, as in a hospital or jail. But a child is physically under the control of his or her caretakers, though less and less so with age. When the child becomes an adult, no one else can make the decisions about his or her thoughts and actions, including the content of and style of communication with others.

The Price of Loss of Autonomy

However, if a child learned that he or she must give away autonomy and self control to others in order to be accepted and loved, that child may become chronically resentful of being in a "one down" position, and grow into an adult who will pick fights with those who make reasonable requests (that are interpreted as orders).

That adult may avoid close relationships (to escape being a self imposed servant to the other person), may become a procrastinator, and may become anxious when dealing with authority in any setting.

This is an area in which Natalie had great difficulty. She attempted, as her mother did, to be totally in control of others in any situation in which she found herself, and being very competent, she could usually function as a leader.

She expended much energy staying "one up" in relationships, at the cost of chronic anxiety over her potential fall into a "one down" position.

She had much experience being dominated by her mother and by her teachers in a rigid religiously oriented private school, so she wanted to be the one in control of others instead of the one being controlled by others.

This is a problem born of the experience of being dominated (or of believing one has to be dominated as the price for being accepted and loved) when learning about autonomy.

Children need the freedom to choose *within limits,* so that they learn how to make their own decisions. Limits describe the areas within which freedom to choose may be exercised, and also describe the areas within which there is no freedom to choose. The limits are essential, so that within the limits, children can experiment with their own freedom and autonomy.

Autonomy in Adolescence

Growing older does not change the fact that a person makes his or her own decisions, within limits. What changes is an expansion of the "world" within which we are free to choose; the limits expand. By the time of late adolescence, the remaining limits are:

1) the limits of physical nature, like gravity, inertia, and lightning. Successful dealing with these limits usually requires some form of cooperation with them, as in "harnessing" electricity to use as a source of power.

2) the limits of social contracts, such as laws and employment agreements. Successful dealing with these normally means honoring our agreements.

3) the limits presented by the fact that other people are not everything we would like them to be. Acceptance of these limits involves accepting others as they are, even when we disapprove of or disagree with them. By affirming the right of the other person to his or her point of view (the only one he or she currently has), we offer the same acceptance we would like for ourselves.

When successful in learning to make decisions and act within limits, a person develops an understanding that marriage, religion, work, and other commitments are an exercise of his or her personal freedom, not a partial or complete sacrifice of that freedom.

3) PEOPLE THINK, FEEL, AND ACT IN THEIR OWN WAY

The *way* we manage our lives is inevitably our own choice, ideally to be affirmed as "good enough for now."

This is the third fundamental psychological principle. Because people are different from each other, genetically, emotionally, and historically, they have different ways of thinking, feeling, and doing things. These differences reflect differences in judgment, which are, in turn, based on life experience.

One couple with whom I worked were on the verge of giving up on each other and getting a divorce. Not that they wanted a divorce; they were simply so tired of verbally fighting with each other and so frustrated at not finding a solution to the same old problem, that they didn't know what else to do. Marriage counseling was their last resort.

Susan's complaint was that Lewis would not respond to what was important to her. Lewis' complaint was that instead of listening to him, she criticized whatever he said or did. They were at an impasse, between their need to be affirmed and their faulty methods of getting that affirmation from each other.

As they learned to listen to each other without being defensive, argumentative, or solving the others' problem, the "crisis" atmosphere between them eased, and the old appreciation of each other began to return. By listening, they communicated awareness of the validity of what the other had to say. By understanding (without necessarily agreeing), they communicated some validation of what the other had to say. By being empathic about the emotional importance of the other's point of view, they communicated affection. By relating in this way, they began to sanctify instead of contaminate the emotional and spiritual space between them.

The Only Judgment We Have Is Our Own

To say one's way is to be affirmed as "good enough for now" is not a stamp of perfection, but an acceptance of the reality that we can only be where we are, not somewhere else. It also implies that no one other than ourselves can chart the course of our lives.

Our own way and our own judgment is the only way and only judgment we have. We can affirm principles proposed to us by parents, religious traditions, political systems, or our own invention, but we are "stuck" with the task of making the decision ourselves about which principles to affirm.

We develop our own value systems, even when the values are handed down to us by others and even though some of them cause us problems after we adopt them. As children, we incorporate some of our values automatically, as we copy our parents or others. Later, as adults, we have the option to modify those values upon which we wish to improve.

Fortunately, we do not have to re-invent everything about living from scratch, since we can learn from others and from great traditions. Yet, we need to know the importance of living our own life in our own way, provided we grant others the same privilege.

This results in the belief that one's own way of doing things is at least "good enough for now" and is sometimes something of which to be proud.

Natalie worked extensively in this area, since she had built her life on the belief that only one way to act, think, and feel was appropriate for any situation, and that her task in life was to find that correct way.

She recreated her entire system of thinking to know that, while one way might be better than another, she would be content to do the best she could at any point in her life, and be pleased to have done as well as she did, with no condemnation of herself or others.

Application of this principle in all areas of her life took several years to accomplish, because it was such an extensive revision of her previous way of living. She used psychotherapy to review and revise her own values, changing decades of belief that achievement of perfection was the only basis on which to relax and enjoy her life.

We Pursue What We Value

When emotionally successful, establishment of the principle of doing things our own way affirms the desirability of persons using their own judgment, charting their own direction in life, of committing to values and a way of life that they choose as best for themselves.

We can develop our own initiative and creativity, while affirming the same right for others to live life in their own way. We can include others in our lives on the basis of mutual consent.

Learning to live life in one's own way takes the form of increased clarity about "wants" and "don't wants," about cooperation with others and sharing. It has to do with empathy and accepting others' ways as different.

It has to do with creativity and problem solving, and with competence, success and failure in achieving goals. It has to do with accepting one's mistakes and failures as "lessons," without devaluing oneself. It has to do with values and the commitment to living out of those values with loved ones and with strangers.

At best, it has to do with choosing to align our lives with the highest values in the universe, in harmony with the spiritual dimension of life, as best we can understand the meaning of that for our own lives.

Integration of Identity in Adolescence

Learning that we do live life in our own way evolves over a longer period of time than the learnings about the first two fundamental principles. While autonomy is becoming fully established, ideally by three or four years of age (with a rehearsal at adolescence), the beginnings of initiative -- pursuing things in one's own way -- are visible, with learning in this area lasting through adolescence.

The process of establishing increased competence in living one's own way doesn't end with the ending of adolescence, though the foundational structure for these abilities will have been put in place by then. Relative competence in all these areas mentioned, and more, will have been accomplished by adulthood, at least in rudimentary form.

Adolescence is a time of integrating this third fundamental learning with the first two and developing a sense of personal identity. The integration process in adolescence is complicated by the last major changes in physiological development: abstract thinking and emerging reproductive sexuality. These three fundamentals form the first third of our pyramid, basic to organizing the rest of one's life.

Abstract Thinking in Adolescence

"Abstract thinking" allows a quantum leap in the ability to manipulate concepts and ideas, based on the brain's development of the capacity to allow viewing a person or idea from an unlimited number of different points of view.

This is the time when seeing oneself in the mirror takes on a new meaning, since we can now see how others might see us as well as how we see ourselves.

Previously, we might have been concerned about how others saw us, but this added ability allows us to imagine ourselves in the other person's shoes, looking back at ourselves. No wonder this adds a new dimension to one's self image!

The new element is the ability to imagine what the other person may be seeing, thinking and feeling as he or she looks at the world. All of a sudden, "how I look to the other person becomes extremely important, since I can (for the first time) imagine the view from his or her perspective." There is the possibility of conceptualizing unlimited possibilities, and analyzing one's own thought process.

The Beginning of Reproductive Sexuality

Add the development of reproductive sexuality to adolescence and there is a task of putting all the emotional learning together that has not occurred before. Since sexuality involves another way of relating to others, including communication on a very personal basis, it inevitably gets the attention of every individual.

Figuring out how to integrate the learnings of the first 10 to 20 years of life is a monumental task that takes time to accomplish, and is part of establishing one's basic personality style. That style is the basis for dealing with the lessons of the rest of one's life, learnings discussed in the next section.

CHAPTER II
FOUR LATER DEVELOPMENTAL LEARNINGS

Four later periods of learning, roughly spanning time periods of ten to twenty years each, have been thought of by Eric Erikson and others as reflecting life's developmental phases, or "crises."

Religious groups provide rituals to mark some of them, as in recognizing movement into adulthood at puberty, marriage ceremonies, baptisms, and funerals. These marker points in living are partly defined by biological changes (e.g., puberty, pregnancy, aging, and death), and partly by economic and psychosocial factors (e.g., marriage, social interests, and occupation).

In each case, the assumption is made here, possibly shared by other psychotherapists, that dealing with the emotional dimension of these developmental tasks in the most positive manner is a desirable goal. Such a belief in the importance of successful accomplishment of these tasks for the development of each individual and for the society at large becomes part of our value system. As human beings and as therapists supporting the growth of others, we have a personal investment in supporting the most positive achievement for ourselves and each individual with whom we work.

The first of the four later developmental learnings has already been introduced in the last chapter, namely identity formation in adolescence. This is the integration of all the learnings previously accomplished, which will usually form the basic personality structure for the rest of one's life. Once the basics are settled in a positive manner, they need not be revisited except for purposes of reevaluation and fine tuning.

The second of the later developmental learnings, establishment of economic independence, flows out of the process of developing the last steps of emancipation from parents and other caretakers. This is a gradual process, and merges with the inner sense of having been financially and socially successful as an adult.

The third later developmental learning, use of creativity as a major contribution to joy in living, evolves naturally from the implicit question, "What shall I do with my independence and abilities?" This is an integration of the certainty of personal competence that began to develop in early school years.

The fourth later developmental learning affirms the value of sharing accomplishments and understandings with others. This is the process of passing on to others what one has learned, the nurturing of the next generation. It also may include a growing awareness of the importance of the spiritual dimension of life, even though that dimension has been a part of life since birth.

These developmental learnings are not "stages" in the sense that one must be completed in order for the next one to occur. Each one evolves long before it becomes a dominant activity and value. But they do tend to emerge consecutively as primary concerns since the accomplishment of success in one major life task encourages and leads to dealing with the next life task. Ultimately each person creates his or her own journey that makes the growth of each person a unique and creative process.

Later Development Needs a Foundation

While no less important than earlier learnings to be achieved, psychological issues dealt with in adolescence and later are built on an earlier foundation, much the same way that the upper part of a pyramid is built on the lower part. Issues to be dealt with in adolescence and later are less basic, yet they are very important in completing personality structure.

The foundation for the individual's personality structure is built in the early years, built on what was learned about the three psychological fundamentals before adult functioning.

The fundamentals established before preadolescence are so important that they color everything that follows. To change them is to change one's personality style and identity. Emotional development during and after adolescence is very important, since later developmental learnings shape the way one's life is lived. But later learnings can often be modified without modifying one's underlying personality structure.

These four later developmental learnings become part of our belief system, in the same way as our beliefs in the first three fundamental assumptions.

1) IDENTITY FORMATION AND SEXUALITY: INTEGRATION WITH THE FUNDAMENTALS

Adolescence is a time of identity integration, of putting the learnings of past years together with emerging erotic sexuality, a task worth accomplishing.

As a functioning individual, each preadolescent already has an identity that has been continuously evolving since infancy. This evolution moves toward a time of more stable integration, using the new ability of abstract thinking to put all the pieces together.

The brain development that allows abstract thinking enables the individual more than ever before to understand the thinking and feelings of others from a new perspective. The adolescent develops the ability to stand in the shoes of others and understand how he or she might appear, looking back from the other person's point of view.

Combining the Social and the Sexual

By puberty, the new experience of physical erotic sexuality must be taken into account and be made an operational part of the individual's self and social system. This may take several years, and varies greatly in different cultures and with differences in the rate of physiological development.

In the cultural context of western civilization, the working out of sexuality occurs at the same time as dating and exploring relationships with others. Ideally, this experience provides an opportunity to clarify the place of sexuality in a close relationship, as part of an understanding of friendship and commitment.

These learnings undergird establishing a longer term intimate relationship with another person as the basis for marriage and mutually shared life. Coupled with sexuality, this mutuality includes the birth of children and the creation of a family.

Ideally, this is the last step in the development of a basis for intimacy, which evolves from the symbiosis of infancy to an increasingly independent way of relating.

Individual independence is a position from which to establish a mutually negotiated partnership, based on the three fundamental beliefs regarding being, choosing, and doing, giving psychological and emotional support for the partner to live on the same basis.

Economic Independence and Responsibility

After identity integration in adolescence, the next task can be understood as establishment of economic independence and responsibility.

Establishing economic independence is not the same as creating an emotional separation from parents and family to establish autonomy, an issue that belongs to earlier developmental work. This is the matter of becoming a peer with one's parents in the fullest sense of adequacy to provide economically and socially for oneself.

One might wonder, "What is left to motivate persons to do anything in life if by the time of mid-teens they no longer must prove (to themselves and to others) their value as persons, having settled that by age two (the first developmental fundamental)?"

And what if they no longer have to prove (to themselves and to others) that they are the manager of their own lives, having settled that by the time they were four (the second developmental fundamental)?

And what if they no longer have to prove (to themselves and to others) that they are entitled to think, feel, and act in their own way, without self-criticism (the third developmental fundamental), having settled that by the time of their late teens?

What if they are relatively "at home" with their sense of themselves as whole persons in relationship with others, including their sexuality?

The answers to these questions are addressed in the discussion of the next developmental learning, which is the process of deciding how to apply one's abilities in the real world, in an economically viable fashion. This is the process of identifying and clarifying areas of activity that give satisfaction at a deep enough level to justify the uninteresting work that is part of most jobs in the marketplace. An important part of this process is the sense of doing something significant as well as economically rewarding, a reflection of inner values and the living out of the spiritual dimension in a pragmatic way.

2) ECONOMIC INDEPENDENCE AND RESPONSIBILITY: MAKING ONE'S MARK IN THE WORLD

Another assumption follows the previous one: it is a desirable, natural and logical next step in individual development to become fully independent by becoming economically self-sufficient. The last step away from dependence on parents or others is that of providing one's own income. Taking responsibility for arranging one's economic independence is as important as how it is done.

This is a familiar issue in psychotherapy, since dealing with present and past difficulties may get in the way of successful and satisfying vocational work in the present. Therapists will agree that earning enough money to avoid being financially dependent on parents or others is a positive contribution to emotional well being.

Selecting an Occupation

A complementary challenge is learning how to prepare for and pursue an occupation so as to make enough money to create an acceptable lifestyle, and at the same time find enough enjoyment in one's work to be satisfied. Emotionally satisfying work is another contribution to emotional well being.

There are various ways to develop the skills to establish economic self sufficiency. In a hunting and gathering culture, those skills might have been learned by an individual in the year or two after puberty rites, sexuality having already been dealt with. In our western civilization it might take the balance of high school or some technical training or college, an extended time to learn how to deal with a more complicated economic system.

The Importance of Children

Sometimes sexuality provides another reality "prod" to become economically responsible, since children normally by our cultural norms have a high value in the eyes of parents, encouraging them to provide the economic necessities. Sexual activity results in children being conceived and born, providing motivation to find the money to take care of them.

What is left to do after the family has "enough" and has a surplus economically? By age twenty five or thirty, a couple may have become parents and may have "made it" financially. What then? If all has gone well emotionally, there may not be the same need to succeed again, based on the same motives of economic independence and responsibility. The life question then becomes: "What shall I do with my surplus time and money? What will be our next undertaking?"

3) CREATIVITY

Creativity is a familiar concept, and may be assumed to have value by many people in addition to psychotherapists. Here it is assumed to be supportive of emotional health.

One answer to the question of what to do with surplus time and money is, "Do something more than provide for necessities. Do something creative."

This idea is an expansion of a theme that begins developing about age three or four. Creativity is a part of many childhood projects. Later, creativity may have been expressed through both job and children. Creativity can be applied to everyday activities, to keep them interesting.

Creativity and Caring for Children

One very challenging and creative task is the provision of a nurturing and supportive environment within which children can develop to their potential. Rearing children is a twenty year (plus) project that demands as much time and energy as parents can allot to it, limited by the need to work in order to earn a living. Nurturing children's growth can be viewed as co-creating with nature, giving continuing satisfaction in each child's unfolding.

Creativity and One's Occupation

At work, having mastered the fundamentals, a person may use creativity as a way to keep a job interesting. If not, a person may have had the urge to go into a related field. When thought of as the process of putting familiar materials together in a new way, creativity can apply to almost any work setting. Creativity may be thought of as a continuing process, to be applied to any type of work, however simple or complex it may be.

For many people work may not be very satisfying, except that it brings a paycheck. It may seem absurd to write about creativity in work, when so much work is pure drudgery, and is not enjoyable, much less a place to exercise creativity. Yet, even in the worst circumstance, ingenuity can be used to find something positive. I remember the experience of an awful job, cleaning out a camp kitchen grease trap cesspool, a disgustingly smelly job. Still, in the midst of the stench, I was enjoying the process of figuring out how to do the job most efficiently, so as to shorten the time I would be in that mess.

Sometimes an improvement in quality does involve moving on to a different, more enjoyable job environment. Such a move may reflect not only the quality of the job, but an evolution in what an individual finds creative and satisfying.

By creating a vision of what is possible, we can pursue a better life. Human beings are imperfect and the vicissitudes of life leave us having made self-limiting compromises along the way. Our work may be one of those areas we enjoy less than we like, something we wish to make more creative. Though it may take time and effort, we can find new ways to create enjoyment in our work.

4) TEACHING AND GIVING TO OTHERS

Another assumption made here is that teaching others what we have learned is deeply satisfying, important for our emotional well being. Having succeeded, we have the urge to teach others the understanding and skills of our success. This activity links us to the rest of humanity, not as caretakers, but as mentors.

Being a Teacher of Others

It is impossible to identify a particular time in life when a person is ready to be a mentor to others. The threads of this capacity lead back to childhood, perhaps to the beginnings of empathy. As part of everyday life, we often teach others and share what we have learned, and find increasing satisfaction in encouraging others to grow and succeed.

Whenever this capacity and desire to share our wisdom with others occurs, we assume it to be a positive, a value to be endorsed and nurtured for the well being of the teacher, for the benefit of the learner, and for the strength of our social fabric.

So another motive and goal remains for all of us, to teach others what we know about making life successful and meaningful, to relieve suffering in whatever ways we can, to devote our energies not only to our own base of operations, our families and work, but to the communities, nations, and world in which we live. When we take care of ourselves, we open the door for caring about others. The best creativity we can muster can be offered out of our resources to those who have less, not to subvert their own process, but to support it, as we would our own children and each other, with the best we know.

The Second Layer of the Pyramid

These four later developmental learnings are the second layer of our "pyramid," resting solidly on the three psychological fundamentals. Affirmation of the three fundamentals provides the essential foundation on which later learning can occur.

Such affirmation forms a solid foundation for successful adult relationships and the pursuit of the four later developmental tasks faced by each person on his or her journey through life.

Beyond the beliefs established by dealing with developmental tasks discussed up to this point, we make assumptions that grow out of our life process, supporting the particular developmental tasks we may be dealing with. Fifteen of these additional assumptions/beliefs are dealt within the next chapter. They do not have the same quality of developmental importance, but may be found cutting across developmental lines, operating in any area or time.

CHAPTER III
FIFTEEN
OTHER ASSUMPTIONS
BASIC TO PSYCHOTHERAPY

In our everyday functioning, personal and professional, we make innumerable assumptions on which we base our thinking, feeling, and behavior. It is impossible to state all of them, but it may be useful to identify some of the most significant as they apply to psychotherapy, in addition to the three fundamentals (and their implications and corollaries) and the four later developmental learnings discussed up to this point.

These fifteen additional beliefs are assumptions that affect the quality of our life, but are not as fundamental as the first three assumptions discussed first, related to being, choosing, and doing. Nor are they as basic as the values that grow out of the four later developmental tasks, accomplished as we move through adolescence and adulthood. They are values that evolve out of the process of living at any stage of development, as a way of making the developmental process more efficient and satisfactory.

Matters of Style and Quality

These fifteen additional assumptions are more like matters of style and quality, that raise or lower the quality of life, depending on the particular beliefs we may choose for ourselves. They are ideas that grow out of and support the first three fundamental principles, assumptions that make the four later developmental tasks easier to accomplish and add to their enjoyment.

They are principles that apply to all the developmental tasks and make their accomplishment more effective. They are abstract concepts that apply to everyday living in very concrete ways. They also color the nature of our spirituality, the way in which we connect to others.

They will be discussed below, even though they may at times seem self-evident, and are proposed as a sampling of values that can raise the quality of life for anyone. These additional fifteen values are arbitrarily chosen from those that are commonly endorsed in psychotherapy. The list is not meant to be exhaustive of all important assumptions, but is only a selection of some values that have common significance. Not every reader will agree with all of them, but hopefully, every person will have a position in regard to them.

While we focus in the following discussion on the values held by the therapist, the values held by the client are equally important, affecting all aspects of everyday living. The values discussed here are thought of in positive terms, values that enhance life. On the other hand, when one's values degrade life, they are destructive, but none the less values. Either way they define the quality of the spiritual dimension of our lives by defining the content of our relationship to others and to ourselves.

1) THERE IS A DIFFERENCE BETWEEN THINKING AND FEELING

One assumption made here is that there is a difference between thinking and feeling.

As far back as 1937, Papez (mentioned by Rossi in *The Psychobiology of Mind-Body Healing*, p. 25) did anatomical research demonstrating "that mental experience was transduced into the physiological responses characteristic of emotions in a circuit of brain structures that constituted much of what is now called the *limbic-hypothalamic system.*" He studied the physiological processes by which our interpretation of events is translated into limbic-hypothalamic "language" that evokes emotional responses from various cells in our bodies.

These studies and others help us understand how everyday experience, thinking and feeling are organically enmeshed, while for purposes of discussion we separate them. However, the way we speak of thinking and feeling may confuse them, if commonly made statements are to be taken seriously.

"Guilty" Is What the Judge Says

We confuse the difference between thinking and feeling when we (including therapists) say, "I feel guilty." We all can agree, upon reflection, that "guilty" is an opinion expressing a judgment, not an affective state of being. As a judgment or interpretation, there are specific feelings that are elicited by the view one holds. The idea, "guilty," might commonly evoke (through the mediation of the limbic-hypothalamic system) the feelings of fear and/or anger.

Yet, when as therapists we use "guilty" as if it is a feeling, we perpetuate the confusion the client brings to the office. It is as if we communicate to the client, "Let's find ways you can modify your unfairly self-critical opinion of yourself, at the same time assuming that self-criticism is not a thought, but a feeling." That would seem to make the work of therapy turgid and more difficult, since we can directly change our mind in ways that we cannot directly change our feelings. That is, we can decide to believe something different. We cannot decide directly to feel something different, since our feelings are connected to and an expression of our interpretation of events (a cognitive process). It seems clearer and more effective to use language that assumes the difference between thinking and feeling.

Feelings Follow Thinking and Behavior

As a practical matter, feelings follow interpretations of events (thinking, conscious or unconscious), so that if we interpret an event as negative ("my boss fired me and I'll never get another job") we may feel angry, scared, and sad. On the other hand, if we interpret an event as positive ("my boss fired me, and now I can get on with my life in a better job"), we may feel pleased and relieved, along with other feelings.

This is a useful way to think of the relationship of thinking and feeling, even though in reality our thinking and feeling is an organic whole, incapable of being dissected and strung out into a linear process.

This powerful effect of thinking upon feeling is the basis of the power of "reframing," changing the interpretive lens through which we look, so as to modify the affective response to the same events. It is also the basis of the power of the technique of EMDR (eye movement desensitization and reprocessing) in reprocessing cognitive information resulting in relief from the panic of unresolved trauma.

2) THERE IS A DIFFERENCE BETWEEN FEELING AND BEHAVIOR

That there is a difference between feeling and behavior is probably easy to agree upon as adults.

There is a time when the magical thinking of the child does not provide differentiation between feeling and behavior. The child may mistakenly assume that anger is dangerous to others because it is associated with fantasies of hurting others, events in which others are hurt, or the hurtful behavior of others.

Or, a child may confuse feeling and behavior when he or she is punished for feeling certain emotions, such as anger or pleasure. For example, a child may be given the message by parents, "Don't be angry," or "Don't be sexual," as if the child can directly control his or her angry feelings or become non-sexual in the same way bodily movements can be controlled. He or she may attempt to control behavior so as to control feelings.

The Difference is Important

So learning the difference between feelings and behavior is an important achievement for children. This clarification leads to important conclusions, like the knowledge that feelings and the thoughts associated with feelings do not cause events to occur. The thought or feeling is not the same as the deed.

For example, a person cannot cause anyone to be hurt by being angry even though the person may wish the other harm. The energy mobilized with anger can be used for destructive behavior, so an angry person may physically hit someone. Or, an angry person may attack someone verbally. Or, on the other hand, the energy generated by anger can be used constructively to solve the problem about which one is angry.

Behavior Includes Treatment of Others

Behavior is directly harmful or helpful. For example, when we treat people badly (behavior) they are hurt by us, but not because of our feelings, our anger. Our behavior, including what we say verbally and express non-verbally, is what hurts or helps others.

When others experience pain in response to being treated fairly, they distort the reality of what the other person has done into something negative. For example, "If you love me you will do what I want" will create pain for the speaker, when the loved one says "no" to the request. The "no" does not create the pain; the pain is self-inflicted by the faulty interpretation of the "no" (which could be: "You don't love me").

The difference between feeling and behavior can also be illustrated with the feeling of fear. Fear does not make a person vulnerable to a dangerous event, nor does fear make a danger more real.

Fear is the feeling response to a *prediction* of imminent danger. The feeling of fear signals us to find a way to avoid possible injury from others or from internal or external events. The fear is not the same as the danger.

Fear is related to behavior in two ways. One way is that when someone else acts (behaves) in ways that seem to endanger our well being, we feel afraid. Our response to that person's threatening behavior is fear. Then the other linkage applies, and we are inclined to do something (behavior) to protect ourselves, since the fear signals that we are in danger. The fear leads to behavior designed to protect us from the danger to which our fear alerts us. Feelings and behavior are related in a very meaningful and useful way, but they are two different things.

3) EMOTIONS PROVIDE POWER TO ACT

This assumption that the energy to act is generated by emotional passion, may be more difficult to clarify, since emotional energy is not something that can be measured or seen.

Our emotions of joy, sadness, anger, and fear vary in intensity. The more intense our feelings, the more we are inclined to do something (behavior) like attacking, submitting, "playing possum" or withdrawing. These are the four primitive modes of self-defense that are genetically build into our brainstem in common with other vertebrates. On the other hand, what we enjoy evokes pleasurable behavior, while what we do not care about evokes little or no feeling, and hence, no emotionally significant behavior.

If I look over my shoulder and see a pit bull type dog bearing down on me while growling ferociously, I will probably conclude (although I don't have to consciously "think about it") I am in danger, feel fear, and be highly motivated to do something to protect myself. I will be highly motivated because self-preservation is emotionally important.

The belief that emotions provide the power to act is an important therapeutic operational assumption for those who believe that people are more willing to change when they have some emotional investment in the process. A client may be motivated to avoid their emotional pain or excited to improve his or her life, or both. An emotional investment in the outcome of therapy increases the odds for success.

Resistance in Psychotherapy

For example, the concept of "resistance" in psychotherapy is based on the belief that fear of being hurt may surface in therapy and thus interfere with the process of therapy itself. Resistance is often spoken of as resistance to change or resistance to the therapeutic process. But at heart, it is resistance to the perceived danger of change; we all recoil from the prospect of more pain. Thus, one of the most important ingredients in successful therapy is the commitment of and determination of the client to achieve change, even if it is frighteningly difficult.

Another illustration of the power of emotion can be found in Transactional Analysis Redecision Therapy. The invitation to change is an invitation to the client to change a lifelong pattern of thinking or behavior. Robert and Mary Goulding, developers of redecision therapy, taught that only a redecision made from the position of the "Free Child Ego State" accesses the emotional commitment of the client. A redecision (thinking) made in association with emotional intensity raises the probability that the change will be implemented and integrated into the client's life style, since emotional commitment requires emotional energy.

Our Passion Reveals Our Values

In a practical way, our feelings provide the emotional energy to act in ways we define as appropriate. When excited, we "jump for joy." When sad, we weep tears of sadness. When angry, we are inclined to assert ourselves in some way. When afraid, we take action to protect ourselves. Whatever we consider to be highly important evokes feelings at a level of passionate intensity roughly proportionate to the importance of the values involved.

The assumption that emotions provide power to act could be stated in many different ways with many qualifications by therapists of various traditions. Yet, we might all agree that emotions play a large role in effecting significant psychological and behavioral change. At times we might even beg the question of the relationship of feelings to change by speaking of emotional change or emotional growth.

At any rate, when we care about someone or something, we pay attention, and the intensity of our feelings roughly approximates the emotional importance of that someone or something.

4) THINKING GIVES US THE ABILITY TO SOLVE PROBLEMS

The assumption that thinking gives us the ability to solve problems may be so well accepted that it needs very little discussion to identify it as a common assumption of therapists. It is probably generally accepted in the culture as basic to problem solving in any work setting.

There was a time in the 1950's when a blue and white sign might be seen on the desk or wall of many executive suites, exhorting anyone who saw it to **THINK.** Yet, some clients stop thinking when they are afraid and do not use their intellectual abilities to deal with a crisis. They may say things like "I just fall apart in a crisis; I get so scared I can't do anything." Or, "I was so scared my mind just went blank."

The Beginnings of Thinking

Our thinking ability emerges quite early, and develops throughout childhood. I can recall with delight my achievement as a toddler when I figured out how the side of my crib could be released to slide downward by pushing a little bar under the bed. Then, with the side lowered, I could climb over and down the side of the crib to the floor, totally proud of myself.

Intelligence allows us to figure things out, and as our physical development brings more mental capacity, we are able to think in more sophisticated ways. By the time a child is twelve or thirteen, the school may provide studies of values and morality, engaging a child's thinking about loyalty, friendship, family, and love. By that time, the child can think about such values as a way to order personal relationships and social intercourse.

Thinking and Psychotherapy

As therapists, we assume thinking is a tool to be utilized for constructive change, no matter how it is seen in relationship to feeling and behavior. When thinking is seriously disordered, we see it as evidence of mental illness, as in schizophrenia, which was first understood as a "thinking disorder" with a common onset in adolescence.

Today, some therapists may say the schizophrenic is thinking more clearly than the therapists. But whatever the discussion, most agree on the assumption that poor thinking (whatever it may be) creates problems, while effective thinking is tool for solving problems.

We can use our thinking to understand that we can use our best efforts to make sense of the process of emotional growth, to understand that no one has the final answers, and that each of us is responsible for our own journey.

5) HUMAN NATURE IS AN ORGANIC WHOLE

We can divide human nature into parts only for the purpose of discussion. Our discussion of the parts does not disconnect them from the whole, any more than our examination of a toe makes it less connected to the body. The assumption follows logically, that human nature is an organic whole.

The same can be said of a family. Examination of the husband's role does not make him less connected to his wife (though one might argue it changes the relationship). Examination of the family's role does not disconnect it from the community, the nation or other families or individuals.

Thinking Systemically

This idea is the assumption underlying family systems thinking, nurtured by Kurt Lewin's field theory and other thinking current in the 1950's and 1960's. Families operate on an interconnected set of beliefs and standard behaviors, that, taken together, form an organic system, and are passed on from generation to generation.

One problem for the therapist is that it is impossible to be simultaneously aware of all aspects of the organic whole, so we must be content to tolerate our inability to attend to the total organism "all at once." When we think about one part, we lose some of our focus on the other parts.

I had a very fortunate experience at about age four. I was playing with my brother (four years older) and his friend. I overheard Gail say to his friend, "Let's do this systematically." Hearing that word, "sys-te-matically," impressed me greatly, and I remember going around for weeks thinking to myself, "Systematic. That's a great way to be. I'm going to do things systematically, figure them out, step by step." That was my introduction to systemic thinking and the organic quality of the universe.

One Application of Systemic Thinking

My training as a pastoral psychotherapist included training in group therapy. My awareness of and commitment to the importance of thinking organically led to my concluding, while in training as a therapist, that in order to be a most effective group therapist, I had the task of being simultaneously aware of:

1) the intrapsychic dynamics of each group member, including each person's personal history and current life situation,
2) the transferential relationship of each person with each group member, in terms of the individual's family of origin,
3) the interpersonal process that developed between each individual and all others in the group,
4) sub-groupings and hierarchies of power,
5) the phase of group development in longitudinal terms,
6) the manifest content being currently expressed,
7) the latent content being currently expressed,
8) the affective position of each person in the group,
9) any evidence of blockage of group movement or resistance to group process, and
10) my own countertransference.

Furthermore, while being aware of all this, I was also to make incisive and timely comments to facilitate the group process and individual growth. I was to make these timely comments in a relaxed and caring manner.

It was clear to me from that time that though the group is an organic whole, I was destined to miss large chunks of it. At such times, a retreat to the fundamentals seemed to me to be the best strategy. One of those fundamentals was to see group members and individuals in relationship, attempting to find a way beyond their self-created pain.

Treatment of the Whole Person

Perhaps is it not too presumptuous to suppose that a large percentage of therapists have as a goal the treatment of the whole person, in the context of their significant relationships and biological determinants, even though we cannot fully achieve the ideal awareness of the whole person.

But we can listen, and understand the parts that are presented and attempt to fit those parts into the organic whole, even though we never fully understand it. The client, in the same way, may be able to understand enough of what is creating the static and suffering in their lives so as to make changes that will be nurturing and life giving.

One of the most destructive things that we do to ourselves is to condemn ourselves for doing as well as we can. This is the subject of the next of our fifteen additional assumptions.

6) CONDEMNATION OF SELF OR OTHERS IS DESTRUCTIVE

That condemnation of oneself or others is destructive may seem so self-evident that it doesn't need to be said, but it is an important operational assumption. Self-condemnation may be the most painful self-imposed emotional experience possible. On the other hand, stated positively, support of and focus on whatever is valued in oneself or others is constructive and desirable. For example, successful parenting requires a continual expression of appreciation of the value of the child(ren) and affirmation of and delight in their growth and activities.

Affirmation of the Positive Instead

In education, the same principle is taught as an approach to learning. Teachers are instructed to help their students build on accomplishments, focusing on what they know and have understood. They are also taught to encourage students to use their already established interests as the platform for further learning, generating excitement for new experiences and accomplishments.

In business management training, courses include the principle of giving employees "positive strokes" for their accomplishments, giving acknowledgment for work well done, rather than criticism for work done poorly. This approach is used because controlled studies have indicated that when this approach is used, productivity rises and the company benefits financially. More advanced managements even have programs that reward employees for identifying problems within the company and discussing possible solutions.

The Development of Self-Condemnation

Albert Ellis provides one view of how people arrive at self condemnation, as part of his thesis that therapists he trains will teach clients how to give up their "absolutistic shoulds, oughts, and musts" (The Evolution of Psychotherapy, pp. 114-115). The following quote spells out the process described by Ellis as the thinking by which a client may arrive at a self-condemning position:

> "Because I *must* succeed at important tasks and *have* to be accepted by significant people, (1) it's *awful* and *terrible* when I fail and get rejected, (2) I *can't stand* failure and rejection, (3) I'm an *inadequate* and *unlovable* person for failing and being disapproved, (4) I'll *always* fail and *never* get accepted, (5) I am so bad that I really don't *deserve* to have a good life and only *merit* continued pain and suffering."

In psychotherapy, whether we subscribe to Ellis' view or not, we may agree with the assumption that self-demeaning thinking is extremely destructive, ideally to be replaced with some kind of self appreciation.

When one or more of the three fundamental values are violated, our guilt notifies us we have "violated our own essential values" and that we need to act to restore our internal integrity.

Shame and Guilt

A study done by Helen B. Lewis in 1971, *Shame and Guilt in Neurosis,* stated a rationale for the therapist's concern for the subject. On page 57, she states:

> "The phenomenological stance toward shame and guilt is not only a source of information about these states but a boon to the therapist and the patient in fostering the patient's acceptance of himself."

The focus of her book is upon an analysis of shame and guilt illustrated with much detailed case material of psychotherapy sessions. The entire study endorses the importance of fostering the patient's acceptance of himself as a goal of therapy. Lewis restates the usefulness of understanding self-hatred at the very end of the book, on page 513:

> "The hypothesis that there are overt, unidentified shame components in depression, and by-passed shame and guilt components in obsessive thinking directs our attention to the process of symptom formation. . . . The therapist's empathetic awareness of this process facilitates the communication and discharge of the self-hatred which is so much the hallmark of neurosis."

Constructive and Destructive Defined

One more comment is necessary regarding this principle, from both a philosophical and practical point of view. A way to summarize the fundamental values being proposed here is to say that whatever is destructive to self and/or others is to be rejected in favor of what is constructive and life-giving. When this principle is violated, our awareness of guilt is very useful in sending an alarm to our system that "something is amiss."

The Therapist's Values

Thus, the therapist may encourage a person engaged in sociopathic behavior, such as sexual abuse, to develop a value commitment that endorses guilt over behavior that is destructive to others. The therapist will encourage the client to reject self destructive shame and self denigration, in effect encouraging the adoption of the value that hurting oneself or others is not acceptable. The therapist has values; what they are becomes clear in the therapy process. The therapist will recommend them in overt or subtle ways to the client.

7) PEOPLE LEARN FROM EXPERIENCE

Another commonly held assumption is that people learn from experience. As a result, we arrange for the appropriate experience when we wish to learn something new.

For example, in order to learn to play the piano, we might arrange to have a piano upon which to practice and contract for piano lessons. To learn to speak Spanish, we might arrange Spanish lessons or travel to a Spanish speaking country.

Learning from Life's Events

Even when we have not planned a learning event, we continue to learn from life experience. What we learn varies; that we learn something is inevitable. One way therapists apply this assumption is by assigning tasks for the client to accomplish between sessions in the hope that the learning flowing from the experienced behaviors will benefit the client.

Much of what is discussed in therapy sessions is the experience of the client, with the goal of gaining new understanding that can be converted into a modification of the client's thinking, feeling, and behavior.

Learning from Birth

We have been learning since we were born (some may say before birth) and continue to learn every day, whether we are 2 months, 20 years, or 80 years old. Debate about whether the past is an important contribution to our learning about living may seem to be a waste of energy, since the meaning we create from past events is inevitably what we use to interpret the present and plan for the future. By viewing the past as events from which we have learned, we can see how those experiences color our understanding and actions in the present.

Learning in Psychotherapy

Periodically, a client will come to a first session of therapy describing a series of failed relationships, saying, "I seem to keep repeating the same mistakes. I must be doing something wrong, and I want to figure out what it is so I can have a relationship that gives the satisfactions I see others enjoying."

It may be difficult at times to "disconnect" the past from the present, and let the past be a memory, instead of a present event, lived over and over. We use the connections of past experience to the present in positive ways, since we cannot “re-decide” everything as we go along. It is inevitable that we use our experience to be effective in the present, acting on “automatic,” as with riding a bicycle. Yet, this creates the difficulty we face when we do wish to change what we do “automatically.”

The Power of State Dependent Memory

A useful way to conceptualize this relationship of the past to the present, taking into account the wholistic, integrated quality of our experience, is that described by Ernest Rossi in his discussion of state-dependent memory, learning, and behavior. In *The Psychobiology of Mind-Body Healing,* he describes state-dependent theory as an integration of four hypotheses (brackets are my comments):

> "1) The limbic-hypothalamic system is the major anatomical connecting link between mind and body.
>
> "2) State-dependent memory, learning, and behavior processes [what we ordinarily refer to as memories] encoded in the limbic-hypothalamic and closely related systems are the major information transducers between mind and body.
>
> "3) All methods of mind-body healing and therapeutic hypnosis operate by accessing [through free association, dream analysis, abreaction, hypnosis, or other means] and reframing [providing a new interpretation of past events] the state-dependent memory and learning systems that encode symptoms and problems.
>
> "4) The state-dependent encoding of mind-body symptoms and problems can be accessed by physiological (e.g., drugs) approaches--and the placebo response is a synergistic interaction of both."

This way of thinking about psychological change accounts for the chemical and biological dimension of our functioning as well as a psychological dimension. It acknowledges the difficulty of change and provides a theoretical framework within which it is possible to develop some ways in which to help change occur.

This theoretical formulation is also supportive of the work Francine Shapiro has developed, based on her book, *Eye Movement Desensitization and Reprocessing.* Her techniques could be understood as one means of reframing the state-dependent memories that encode symptoms and problems. Her work has been so well researched that EMDR is now considered the treatment of choice for trauma victims.

8) HUMAN BEINGS ARE SOCIAL ANIMALS

Another generally held assumption about human nature is that people are inclined by more than economics to seek contact with each other, to arrange to live in families, small groups, or tribes of families. The social nature of mankind is taught in introductory sociology as basic to human relationships: "Human beings are social animals."

Isolation is not the preferred state for emotional satisfaction and health. This is particularly clear when considering the general anxiety found in people facing potential or actual rejection by others. Fear of rejection or abandonment is a common clinical concern on the part of many clients, and therapists as well.

The inclination of people to connect and be in relationship with each other can be understood as evidence of the spiritual dimension of life. At the very least, the spiritual dimension implies connectedness of all things, especially people with each other. This connection begins before birth, and is formulated in myriad ways throughout the development of each individual.

Our desire for contact with others can be seen as a movement toward intimacy, limited by the pain created by difficulties in relating. What may be much less clear is how much intimacy is desirable. People vary in the degree of intimacy they choose and in the ways they use to achieve closeness.

Degrees of Closeness

The question of the degree of intimacy is the same as "How close do I want to be?" The answer to that question may be something like "I want to be as close as possible without being smothered (fundamental value number one) or dominated (fundamental value number two), or told how I must do things (fundamental value number three)," the particular concern being defined by the issue where the person is growing emotionally.

But these kinds of answers confuse the *degree* of closeness with the *basis* on which closeness is achieved. "How close" is a matter of degree. "How close" is not a basis for closeness, is not the principle on which closeness is established.

The Basis for Closeness

Closeness can be based on symbiosis and enmeshment, which raises the fear of being engulfed by the other person. Or, closeness may be based on the submission of one person to the decisions of another, evoking the fear of being dominated. Or, closeness may be based on the premise, "There are many ways to do something and my way is the correct way," leading to resentment over loss of one's own initiative.

A preferable basis for intimacy can be found in affirmation of the separation between individuals, an acknowledgment that each person decides for himself or herself, and acceptance of the differences found in others, leading to mutual affirmation. But, the *way* one is close is very different from the *degree* of closeness.

Our Need for Connection with Others

The need for communication and contact with other human beings is a need we never outgrow, much like the need for food and water for physical sustenance. The idea that a nurturing type of personal contact is essential for health and well being is plausible when we look at the great amount of attention given to maintaining and improving personal and social relationships. It is also a way to understand the exchange of energy between people that begins with conception and continues in various forms throughout life. This exchange of energy can be thought of as the spiritual connection people make with each other.

Social commentary confronts us with the importance of the quality of personal relationships. We are told in books, the newspaper, and political speeches that "The family gives stability to the society." Studies conclude that single older people live longer when they have a pet or a social group to whom to relate. The same point is repeated over and over: we need relationships in order to thrive. In evaluation of clients, a standard psychoanalytically oriented diagnostic question is, "Tell me about your close friends when you were growing up."

It seems reasonable to think most therapists would agree that human beings are inclined to communicate and share experiences with others, and that positive social contacts contribute to emotional health.

9) WE ALWAYS SELECT WHAT WE SAY AND DO

Another premise that may be generally accepted is that we cannot say everything simultaneously. Since this is true, we must select for actual communication the small part of everything that we could or would like to say in a given moment.

One of the important discoveries Freud made was that if a person does not consciously attempt to select what to say (free association), his or her unconscious does the selecting and a theme of emotional importance emerges.

We Select What We Say

Consciously or unconsciously, we know that saying something is not the same as saying everything. So we select what we say spontaneously or at other times select what we say self-consciously and carefully to serve the particular purposes we have in mind. We each have our own criteria for selecting what we say, whether the process is unconscious or we are aware of those criteria.

At times we even give contradictory messages, one consciously through our verbal message, and the other out of our awareness through non-verbal means. We select what we say in some fashion and communicate a discrete meaning through our own style.

Some studies suggest that the majority of what we communicate is through "body language," a lesser amount through facial expression and our tone of voice, and a still lesser amount through the verbal content of what we actually say. Our communication will "leak out," whether we intend it to or not, by whatever means it is delivered.

Therapists Also Select What They Say

Since everyone communicates in these several ways, it follows that therapists also communicate in the same ways. The content of therapeutic communication is selected on the basis of criteria of which the therapist may or may not be aware. Even if our utterance is a totally spontaneous issue from our unconscious, we still select what to say unconsciously, without thinking about it in a self-conscious manner, and what we say is intended to communicate a particular set of meanings.

Perhaps it is an acceptable corollary, discussed more fully later, that it is desirable be aware of one's criteria for communication. This addresses the issue of countertransference for the psychotherapist.

But even if the idea of unconscious selection is rejected in favor of conscious or pre-conscious selection of what we say and do, the same point is made: we select what we think, say, and do *in some way*, in or out of our awareness.

We're in Charge of Our Own Message

This assumption gives responsibility for clear communication to the individual who is doing his or her communicating and acting. It also empowers us to be intentional in our communication and behavior.

By acknowledging that each of us is in charge of our own communication and behavior we can take responsibility for modification of what we say and do according to objectives we have in mind. For example, if we decide to create enemies, we can attack others, verbally or physically. If we decide to create friendly or loving relationships, we can treat others in positive and affirming ways.

While we may not always be so intentional in our approach to or response to others, we always have the option to do so if we wish. We can act in ways that are benevolent and constructive. When we are not sure how to do that, we can find ways to learn how to do so.

However we communicate, it will be an expression of our spiritual connection to others. How we operate spiritually may be beyond our immediate control, but is and will be an expression of all that we are. As such, the categories of conscious and unconscious do not apply. Rather, out of our organic unity, we will express who we are and how we connect to others in a way that can be understood as a spiritual communication.

10) WE ARE ALWAYS DOING SOMETHING

A familiar dialogue is attributed to children's quest for personal space: "Where have you been?" "Out." "What did you do?" "Nothing."

While frustrating at the time it happens, the humor in this exchange makes the point. The assumption here is that we cannot do nothing. We are always doing something. This area of discussion, that we are always doing something, may be an area of some controversy, since it touches on the third fundamental assumption discussed earlier, whether it is acceptable for people to do things their own way, differently from others.

What a client "does" defines in a major way what his or her life will be. The choice is not *whether to choose* about eating, smoking, sexuality, treating others well, and so on, but *what the choice will be.* Each person is free to choose, inevitably makes choices, and lives with the consequences of the choices.

What the Psychotherapist is Doing

As psychotherapists, we are also always doing something, even if we are being quiet. Therapists differ markedly from each other in the way they do therapy, in their techniques. It is clear from the broad spectrum of therapeutic methodology that creative individuals have and will go on inventing new ways of doing therapy.

Techniques have to do with what we do to accomplish a goal, so our options in developing techniques are somewhat limited. But when creating theoretical formulations, the possibilities seem less limited.

For example, there may be some finite number of ways in which to communicate to others, but an infinite number of ways to think about communication. It may be that the invention of new methodologies will be mostly a refinement of methods already being used, just as modern microsurgery is a refinement of older, cruder methods, even though we will continue to be surprised by new techniques.

However much we may differ on opinions about the relative effectiveness of various technical maneuvers used in psychotherapy, we can all agree that the therapist will do *something*. Once that is accepted, the question becomes what to do in ways that hold promise of being most constructive and therapeutically healing.

We use our judgment and thinking ability to plan what to do, implementing our planning by translating the plan into behavior.

11) WHAT WE DO AFFECTS OTHERS

One challenge all psychotherapists face, then, is to choose *what to do* with clients, whether to be passive or active, see people individually, as couples, families, groups, or some other way, whether to use one technique or another, and so on. The assumption here is that whatever the therapist does or says will affect the client's cognitive, emotional and behavioral system, for good or ill. Therapists have the goal and the responsibility to use criteria that are as constructive as possible for deciding what to say or do.

The principle that what we do affects others applies equally to the ways a client may change in the process of therapy. Thinking and behavior go together to create a powerful combination, in which the "payoff" is the positive change in the client. Behavioral change will also stimulate others to respond to the client differently. Additionally, behavioral change creates a modified internal experience for the one making the change.

We Choose Our Responses

We are in charge of the non-physiologically determined responses we make to inner and outer stimuli, and can modify our responses to some degree. Most psychotherapists might agree with this assumption, since therapists are in the business of helping people change by saying and doing what affects their ways of thinking, feeling, and acting.

Even a therapist's passivity has a powerful effect on a client, as has been long understood by psychoanalytic theory and practice. A therapist's silence encourages transference, a response to the therapist based on and distorted by the client's historical relationships.

We Stimulate, Not Cause A Response

While we are not responsible for what others think, feel, and do, we do have an effect upon others. Whatever we do within the sensory range of another person affects that person to the extent he or she perceives the stimulus we put out. The other person has no choice about whether to respond (unless the stimulus is screened out in some way), but does have some choice about how to respond, within biological limits.

This idea can clarify some confusion about whether one person can control another. One way to think about control is to review fundamental assumption number two, that each person is in charge of himself or herself, like it or not. The only time we control others is when we take physical control, as with children, or as in a jail. Other than these exceptions, we literally cannot control others' thinking and emotions.

Prediction is Another Matter

While we cannot control what others do, think, or feel, since they are in charge of themselves, we can use our abstract thinking ability to *predict* (with varying degrees of certainty) what others *may* do, think, or feel. This is the ballpark of stimulus and response, not cause and effect.

When we are excellent predictors, we may create the illusion of control of others by predicting what they will do, though we are actually still playing the odds. This is the reason to get acquainted with others, to have some idea what to expect from them. This is the same as predicting what they will be like in various circumstances.

We know that, since what we do affects others, we can estimate what that response *might* be. We put out a stimulus, and others *must* respond, even though they are free to select their particular response. Since we are always doing something (assumption #10), we select the way we think and what we do (assumption #9) so as to affect others in a predictable way.

So we have the option of intentionally choosing positive ways of relating to another person. When others respond in positive ways, we can do more of what results in a positive response. When others respond negatively, we can modify our thinking and behavior. The question of what is positive or negative leads to another question: what are the most positive or negative criteria on which to base our choice of behavior?

12) WE USE VALUES AS CRITERIA FOR ACTION

Just as we cannot choose to do nothing, we cannot function without values we use as criteria for action. The ordinary decisions a therapist makes are assumed to be based on some consideration of what is "constructive" or "helpful" and what the client is doing that is "constructive" or "destructive." These decisions are based on the therapist's values.

We Are Constantly Choosing What To Do

The choice by a therapist of what to say is based on an implicit set of values about what may be helpful. Just listen? Confront gently? Make a provocative comment? Ask for more clarification? Suggest an exercise? Make a significant point? All these options, and more, reflect ongoing *evaluation* of the therapeutic process, and selection of what to do, based on that evaluation.

Evaluation Requires Values

Therapists may not always be aware of the particular criteria that influence their interventions with clients. Thus, therapy may be referred to as an "art." Or the therapist may be described as acting out his or her countertransference, unaware of the process. Even when the therapist is not aware of the criteria being used, they exist and reflect his or her values.

Some therapists pay attention to what they believe and how those beliefs may affect their clients, assuming that what they say has considerable impact on their clients. How that self-awareness will be used is a matter of choice, depending on the frame of reference of a particular therapist.

Varieties of Values

Some therapists, impatient with intrapsychic considerations, may analyze the intra-system dynamics. Others, impatient with any analysis, may focus on changes in behavior. Others will primarily utilize hypnosis or EMDR to bypass the conscious mind and deal with emotional issues more directly.

These and other positions reflect the use of different techniques to pursue objectives based on values about what is positive for particular clients, hopefully closely related to the realities of human nature and social functioning, but values, nevertheless.

Clients Also Act On Their Values

Clients also direct their own actions, based on their values. One way of understanding some of the problems clients present in therapy is to see them as reflections of values that are currently misplaced. For example, the man who values emotional coldness as evidence of his strength will have painful experiences in close relationships when his partner demands emotional warmth. As he reconsiders the meaning of strength, he might redefine it to include the ability to express emotional warmth, or at least to express feelings.

In a humorous “spaghetti western” movie made in the 1950's, the cowboy gunfight hero responded with a long pause to his son's query about whether he was scared, and then said, "Yup." This fundamental values shift, redefining thè meaning of a man in the West, is what this father in the movie was teaching his son.

Values are with us to stay, and clients who change their personalities and ways of doing things change some values in the process.

13) IT IS DESIRABLE TO BE AWARE OF OUR VALUES AND BELIEFS

The statement that "those who are unaware of history are destined to repeat it" has a grain of truth in it. Perhaps the grain of truth is that we use what we know from past experience to deal with the present.

We can learn from the past and use that experience to modify and improve the way we deal with similar situations in the present. From our experiences, we develop a framework of beliefs and values about living, about what "works" and what doesn't "work." Although they are learned, we may or may not be self-consciously aware of our values and beliefs.

We Do What We Have Learned to Do

Learnings from the past affect the way we live in the present. Michael Yapko, a clinical psychologist who uses hypnosis to treat people with depression, wrote in his book, *When Living Hurts,* on pp. 48 and 49, that:

> "The individual value system one incvitably acquires during the socialization process is a composite of many inputs from diverse sources. It is the author's belief that it is the person's value system more than any other single factor that is the greatest determinant of what one is and is not able to do. The process of learning to make sense out of a potentially overwhelming world of experience involves internalizing thoughts and feelings about what is right or wrong, normal or abnormal, good or bad, and so forth. These are the value judgments that serve to define the limits of experience."

The Therapist Has Values and Beliefs

It is desirable to be aware of our own values and beliefs. The psychotherapist, by being clear about his or her own values, is able to use them to support the client's positive goals in therapy. By being aware, the therapist is able to address the client's issues with understanding and technical resourcefulness. The therapist can also protect the client by acknowledging the biased nature of his or her point of view, especially when it relates to decisions the client must make.

Said another way, the more one knows about one's own values and faith stance, the more one will be listening effectively and communicating clearly to others. Since psychotherapy has much to do with methods of listening and understanding and communicating with clients clearly, self-understanding provides a knowledge base from which to teach others.

The Client Has Values and Beliefs

The client also does well to be aware of his or her value assumptions, since they will affect decisions made whether or not awareness is present. To be aware of one's values and their connection to decisions opens one to options that would not otherwise be considered.

For example, a woman who is clear that she deeply wants to bear a child will pursue options to make that possible. Denial of that self-awareness for the sake of avoiding conflict with a fiance or husband may result later in painful marital conflict because of her sacrifice.

All of the significant issues dealt with in therapy can be viewed through the lens of the client's value system and how it affects his or her thinking, feeling, and behavior.

14) SYMPTOMS ARE SOLUTIONS

Symptoms are "the best solutions a person could create given the context and people available." This is another assumption, perhaps one with which most therapists would agree.

One application of this principle is found in the "strategic" approach to therapy, since a change in one part of the interpersonal system as directed by the therapist has a powerful effect on the rest of the system. A change in the system will affect the underlying dynamics of the individuals in the system and the way they relate, without the necessity of focusing on the dynamics directly.

Seeing Symptoms as Solutions Affirms the Power to Change

For example, when a couple learns to listen to each other and communicate their understanding, instead of immediately attempting to fix the problem or instead of becoming argumentative, they positively affect the relationship without analyzing anything. Their success or failure in maintaining a positive relationship is the evidence of their decisions about how to treat each other, their solutions to the problems they experience with their partner. By revising their ways of treating each other, their "symptoms," they may solve their "problems."

Seeing symptoms as solutions also implies that developmental growth is possible, that what "works" at one stage of development may be only partially adequate as growth continues, calling for additional adaptation. What might have once been the best possible solution under the circumstances may not be as acceptable in a different time and place.

What was once a "solution" may later become a "symptom." For example, being a good boy or girl may be appropriate at age three or four in a way that would not be suitable at age thirteen or fourteen, or at age twenty three or twenty four.

The assumption that psychological symptoms are ways of solving problems places responsibility for the symptom with the person creating the solution/symptom, allowing for the possibility of a new solution.

The Power to Change Resides in the Client

In the context of psychotherapy, the responsibility for selecting what changes to make rests with the client. The client is the one who implements those changes.

Another way of expressing this same principle is stated by Michael Westerman, in his article "A Hermeneutic Approach to Integration: Psychotherapy within the Circle of Practical Activity," in the *Comprehensive Handbook of Psychotherapy Integration*:

> "The hermeneutic philosophical perspective suggests an approach to psychotherapy aimed at helping patients make changes in the action patterns that make up how they live their lives. That is, the central focus is on patterns of action, not on how patients think about themselves and the world, nor on specific problematic behaviors -- although cognitions and behaviors have a place within the general framework. This viewpoint follows directly from the idea that the person's involvement in the world of practical activities is the touchstone" (p. 92).

Whether viewed clinically or theoretically, the central point is that behavior and behavior patterns define the relative success individuals and groups accomplish in everyday living and relationships.

What a person does to better his or her own life is the "bottom line."

15) NO THEORY OR TECHNIQUE IS ULTIMATE

Many exciting developments continue to occur in the field of psychotherapy. One example is the development of the theory and practice of EMDR, Eye Movement Desensitization and Reprocessing. The development of new methods and theory in psychotherapy is a sign of health and creativity.

No matter how wonderful or useful a new theoretical framework or technical approach to treatment, they are no more than that: new, wonderful, and useful. Creating the ultimate theory or developing the ultimate technique is still a goal and not an achievement.

Perhaps most therapists will agree with this assumption, except for those who are emotionally invested in having their own school of therapy be the most generally accepted and valued.

For those not ready to agree with this assumption, it may be informative to reminisce about the history of psychoanalysis as an illustration of a once dominant theory and technique that is no longer dominant. It is also interesting to note that the most incisive critics have not been able to destroy the significance of the seminal contributions of Freud regarding the unconscious, dreams, and free association.

Varieties of Psychotherapy

As we have more reliable therapeutic outcome studies, we will be able to expand our consensus on ways to think about and conduct the most effective psychotherapy for specific emotional conditions. But ultimate understanding will elude us for some time to come. Until that time, we may be able to agree that all can have something to contribute.

Writers estimate that there are over 300 theoretical models of psychotherapy. The twenty seven writers included in the collection of essays, *The Evolution of Psychotherapy,* published in 1987, are all different from the fifty writers included in *The Comprehensive handbook of Psychotherapy Integration,* published in 1993.

Fifty seven additional different authors are included in *The Clinical Psychology Handbook,* published in 1983. The point illustrated is that variety is the norm, and that each of the writers present their own different theoretical slant.

Varieties of Clients

Similarly, each client's way of thinking and acting is not exactly like anyone else's. As long as these differences do not subvert fundamental values, like criticizing, demeaning, or shaming others, the many differences in ideas and style of behavior can be what make others interesting and desirable to be around.

As an operational principle, the most desirable models we have for thinking, feeling, and acting are not the final word, but stations along the way, allowing for creation of new understanding as the norm to be endorsed. This can also be seen as a spiritual position, affirming that the truth is larger than any of us, and is to be pursued though never fully captured.

NOTE ON VALUE ASSUMPTIONS:

BELIEFS: A PRAGMATIC FAITH

Up to this point we have discussed the three value assumptions that grow out of human development in the first few years of life. This is the first third of our pyramid of beliefs, the foundation. We have discussed the four value assumptions that grow out of an individual's social development after adolescence. This forms the second third of our pyramid of beliefs, the middle section, planted firmly on the foundation.

We have also discussed fifteen other assumptions that make the process of living more understandable and manageable. They complete the final third of our pyramid of beliefs, the upper section that is not so foundational but still significant in forming a lifestyle.

All of these assumptions can be demonstrated as having validity in various ways, but cannot be proven to be true in the scientific sense, with controlled studies, and so on. One of the ways to illustrate their lack of scientific verification is the fact that any one of them may generate a lively debate as to it's validity and usefulness as a guideline for living.

The Meaning of Faith

Since these operational beliefs are debatable, it seems reasonable to think of them as a kind of "faith," not arrived at blindly, as in believing in things we cannot understand, but just the opposite, as believing what seems from life experience to be valid and trustworthy, even though not universally affirmed by everyone.

It is interesting to note that the Greek word for "faith" is a noun, *pistis*. The way the word is used gives it the meaning "that in which I believe." The Greek word for "believe" is a verb, *pistevo*, another form of the word for faith, *pistis*. So, in Greek, the language of the New Testament Bible, there is only one root word for both faith and believe. The position taken here is the same as the Greek meaning, that our faith is that in which we believe. This is an arbitrary definition, but no more arbitrary than the Greek language.

In the last two chapters of the book, we will explore two areas related to our faith assumptions and their application.

The focus in chapter IV will be on how we can think of our value assumptions and beliefs as our faith, defined as that which we consider to be most "high" and most "real." We will also explore the way in which the therapeutic process is an inevitable part of the spiritual dimension of life.

In the following chapter V, we will examine some ways that values and beliefs are applied in clinical practice, illustrated in the use of various therapeutic techniques.

CHAPTER IV
THE FUNDAMENTALS AND OTHER BELIEFS VIEWED AS FAITH

I was meeting recently with Ned, discussing his struggle for affirmation of his professional work. He was having difficulty hearing others criticize his way of doing things, even though he was sure his way was preferable.

When I told Ned he could expect that, in time, he would find it easier to let others hold a different position, he said, "Yes, just like when we started, I didn't mind lying about things, and manipulating people, and had difficulty getting used to being direct and truthful.

“But now, misleading others just isn't acceptable to me, and when I or anyone else leans in that direction, I sense it and my alarm goes off. Now, nothing is more important than my integrity."

Ned had modified his faith. Before, his faith was, "Manipulate others before they manipulate you. If you bend the truth in the process, so be it. Whoever is better at outwitting others wins."

His emotional issues ran deep, to early childhood when he concluded nonverbally that no one would be there to take care of him, that he could depend on no one. So his therapeutic work was difficult, and took years to accomplish since he had difficulty "depending" on the therapist not to disappear. But now, his faith reads, "Be honest, clear, and make agreements fairly. Treat others the way you would like to be treated. This way to live is more rewarding than any other."

Ned's new faith respects the value of the other person and his or her right to make choices freely, even if they are not the choices he would prefer. This approach captures the three fundamental values discussed in this book. These three fundamentals, the four later learnings, and the fifteen other beliefs are assumptions, articles of faith, something we may choose to believe because they appeal to what is most high and real in our own experience. We do not fully achieve them, even though we may pursue them as desirable goals.

A Definition of Religion and Faith

The view presented here is consistent with the thinking of Nels Ferré, once professor of philosophical theology at Vanderbilt Divinity School. He has defined religion as our commitment to *what we consider to be most high and most real (Faith and Reason).*

Using this definition, our faith is our commitment *to believe in* what we consider to be most high and most real, some of which may be "provable" and some not. The meaning of faith is not limited to belief in the unprovable.

Faith includes belief in what can be empirically validated through scientific means, as with our faith that the world is round. Most of us do not understand how to prove the world is round, but we believe it is round anyway, because others say they have traveled around the world and because we see the news reports on TV of the astronauts circling the globe. We believe what others have validated for us.

Faith is not used here to refer to or imply a connection with any organized religion, though religious groups speak about matters of faith. Here the word, faith, is used in the generic sense to describe what we all must believe in order to function as persons and as therapists. We have to believe something in order to function as therapists. We adopt certain operating assumptions as "true."

Some of these assumptions are based on evidence that support their validity, such as the world being round or experience that infants need to be picked up and held in addition to being fed and clothed, in order to be healthy. Other assumptions may be more difficult to support empirically. We build what we believe into an operational framework of faith assumptions even though we do not normally call our beliefs "faith," unless we also believe in a "higher power."

Alcoholics Anonymous and Values

Alcoholics Anonymous has done much, perhaps as much as any movement, to make discussion of a higher power acceptable in therapeutic circles. As Howard Clinebell puts it in his book:

> "This need is for a growing relationship with the divine Spirit, whose acceptance of you has no strings attached and whose love is always

> available to heal your brokenness and liberate you to live and love more fully. The very heart of spiritual growth work is learning how to open our lives to become more receptive to the healing, cleansing energy of God's love (*Well Being,* pp. 25-26)."

One interpretation of this idea is to see it as a projection upon the image of God the love a mother ideally has for an infant. On the other hand, it is equally logical to say that God's love for creation is eloquently reflected in the love of a mother for her infant. Either way, love wins.

Dysfunctional Beliefs and Behavior

A way to understand some of the difficulties of the clients we see when working as therapists is to understand they are suffering from dysfunctional beliefs, faith in ways of viewing themselves and others, and ways of relating, that bring them unwanted and unpredicted dysfunctional consequences.

We are all faced with the irony that, even in rejecting the three fundamentals, four later learnings, and fifteen beliefs described here in favor of other assumptions, we would be acting on faith, since the alternative assumptions cannot be proven, either. We give allegiance to whatever we make the operational foundation of our psychotherapy, (and our life) without being able to prove it is the ultimate truth.

Faith Assumptions and Society at Large

Allegiance may seem to be a strange word to use in association with psychotherapy, but it expresses the connection between values and action. For example, Thomas Jefferson, who wrote most of the U.S. Declaration of Independence, states (brackets mine): "We hold these truths to be self-evident [an act of faith], that all men are created equal, that they are endowed by their Creator [religious faith] with certain unalienable Rights, that among these are Life [being], Liberty [choice], and the pursuit of Happiness [thinking, feeling, and doing things one's own way]."

As dramatic and powerful as this statement is, and was in 1776, it was a concept rising above its own time, with "men" still being taken literally as excluding women and blacks (as the property of the men in power) from the vote. Allegiance to these higher values had not yet been translated into action changing the social status of women and blacks.

It was not until the 1910's for women and 1960's for blacks that they were allowed to fully exercise their right at the national level to make decisions politically through voting. Blacks did not escape slavery until after 1865 and the conclusion of a bitter and tragic war. Children are only now being recognized socially as individuals in their own right, deserving the same respect as other, older persons. Translating values into individual and social behavior may take a long time.

Another application of these values is made by Thomas Szasz, M.D., who makes a powerful case for the importance of autonomy and the right of persons to do things their own way, illustrating historically how the religious tradition of Christianity used the political power of the state for denial of individual freedom.

He describes how, as the practices of the church in the early 16th Century became intolerable to clergy such as Martin Luther, the ". . . Protestants--the name is important--protested against two things: indulgences and the Inquisition. The former symbolized fraud, while the latter symbolized persecution, both practiced, of course, in the name of God." (The Evolution of Psychotherapy, Jeffrey K. Zeig, ed, pp. 420-421).

This counter-attack in favor of individual freedom was not securely established by the time of the writing of the U.S. Constitution, but the principles were written there, in the first amendment and in the balance of power structured into the three branches of government.

Thus, the establishment of religious and political freedom was only beginning by the 18th Century. Dr. Szasz makes the point in his chapter that the psychiatric/political alliance is still struggling with the issue of how much freedom to allow those who do not think in ways that are generally accepted by the cultural consensus.

Summary

The issues of 1) the value of each individual, 2) individual autonomy and 3) freedom to think and live one's own way are fundamental to human nature, even when, and perhaps especially when they are denied.

They are three of the most basic articles of faith we may share in common as psychotherapists. We participate in the process of applying these values to living through the way we live our own lives and in the way we treat our clients.

The four other beliefs in 4) the importance of personal identity, 5) economic independence, 6) creativity, and 7) service to others are not as fundamental as the first three. They are more fundamental than the fifteen other assumptions. But, to the extent any of the assumptions are affirmed, they are articles of faith to be supported in psychotherapy.

The idea that faith is part of the therapy process may seem incongruous to some, and natural to others. It is an issue of importance worthy of some discussion.

1) PSYCHOTHERAPY AND FAITH

One medical doctor, describing the importance of the way he views and communicates with his patients, said "The most important questions I ask my patients are, 'Where does it hurt?' and 'How bad is it?'" People come for help because of their pain, hoping to be listened to, taken seriously, and helped.

One implication of proposing any kind of "therapy" is that it will be a help to the person receiving the therapy. It is an aid to return to a previous level of functioning, or in some cases, to improve one's level of functioning toward a goal that seems possible.

Two Motives for Personal Improvement

In the first instance, that of returning to a previous level of functioning, a person might receive physical therapy after a broken ankle, in order to reclaim use of the ankle as enjoyed before the break. The physical therapy is meant to support the potential healing inherent in human nature.

In the second case, that of developing toward a desired objective, a physical therapist might be employed in a training camp to assist athletes to improve their physical functioning, relative to the sport for which thcy are training. The goal would be to improve the level of functioning beyond what was enjoyed before, in terms of the criteria of the designated sport.

In the same two ways, psychotherapy may be of aid with emotional issues. In the first instance, a psychotherapist may assist a client to regain a previous level of functioning. For example, a man who finds himself increasingly unwilling to drive his car with panic may seek psychotherapy to remove his phobia of driving. When he has dealt with that disruptive symptom and has reclaimed his ability to drive without disabling fear, he may stop therapy.

In the second instance, having become more aware of his pervasive "background" fear of being dominated by others, he may wish to continue therapy for the purpose of developing more satisfying close relationships. Or a woman may contract for therapy to change a long term pattern of choosing to be close to men who reject her. Here the movement is toward a positive goal in addition to relief of pain.

Such improvements in quality of life require dealing with values and beliefs that in turn, affect the way a person feels, thinks, and relates to others. These are issues therapists address, whether or not they think in terms of values and faith.

Psychotherapy as a Faith Journey

An Adlerian psychotherapist, Harold Mosak, put the matter of faith in therapy in traditional religious terms, as if he were a clergyperson in some religious community. In his chapter in *What is Psychotherapy,* Jeffrey Zeig, ed., he says on p. 27 (brackets are mine):

> "My goals vary with the patient. I listen to confessions, extend hope, relieve guilt, 'heal' the sick, raise the fallen, lift up the spirit, illuminate and unravel 'the mysteries,' propose new options and alternative behaviors, and promote faith. The patient's growth of faith in my religion promotes growth of faith in self--the feeling that they are worthwhile as they are [first fundamental]. They learn the courage to be imperfect ...and they learn that imperfection renders them merely human and capable of belonging [third fundamental]."

> "What I do is not science. The therapist is an artist, often a charismatic one, who is proficient in matters of faith enhancement. While the 'conversion process' is not science, it is nevertheless amenable to scientific investigation."

The Therapeutic Contract

When a psychotherapist and client begin the process of therapy, they make some explicit or tacit agreement about the goals to be accomplished. To set goals, both psychotherapist and client must use some criteria in defining desirable change to be accomplished in therapy.

All therapists have criteria for deciding what they do with clients. The particular plan cannot be empirically proven as valid, yet is an inevitable basis for doing psychotherapy, anyway. The client and therapist arrive at mutually acceptable criteria for change in some manner, and that shapes the effectiveness of the course of therapy.

Some criteria are built into the client's request for help. One criterion is reduction of emotional distress, such as anxiety, depression, or excessive anger.

Typical Requests for Help

As an example, Janet recently came to my office complaining of panic attacks that were so severe that she had been to the emergency room of the local hospital several times. As she dealt with her fear of dying if she were rejected by her husband, she became more secure and her anxiety diminished.

Janet was preoccupied with reading her supervisor's mind so that she could respond with what he wanted before he asked. That was her old way of avoiding rejection by him, making her job very stressful and seemingly dangerous.

As she continued to see herself as a separate person with something of value to offer in her own right, able to take care of herself "on her own," her relationships became more satisfying, and she began to enjoy living her life without the constant emotional drain of worrying about who might be displeased.

Another type of request for help may be the removal of symptoms that interfere with desired daily functioning, such as compulsive behavior that makes doing one's job more difficult. Or a client may want to cancel his oppositional behavior that invites rejection from others. Or low sexual desire may be a problem that creates conflict in a marital relationship.

Other requests for help may be related to an improvement in quality of life, described as a decrease in loneliness, more satisfaction in relationships, or a greater ability to feel or play.

As therapy proceeds from the presenting symptoms to other concerns, all three types of requests for help are touched -- removing emotional distress, improving everyday functioning, and improving the quality of life.

When the Authorities Take Over

What about "enforced therapy," the forcible placing of individuals in mental hospitals as used for social control? This is, in effect, a forcing upon the patient the criteria of the therapist.

At the very best, it is a relatively benevolent method of protecting others from a perceived threat to their life, liberty, or pursuit of happiness, the three fundamentals not open to debate. At its worst, it is a threat to those fundamentals.

This issue is important enough to mention here, not only for those who manage people deemed not able to manage themselves without being self or other-destructive. It is an issue for every person. It is an issue of human nature, whether anyone does well to compromise these three fundamentals. This matter is worth noticing, though it will not be debated here.

The proposal here is that even when focusing on symptom removal, and especially when contracting with a client to help improve his or her quality of life, the therapist operates on the basis of the assumptions described so far, integrated in some way as part of the therapist's personality.

These assumptions are understood here as articles of faith, believed to be true as operational principles or values, especially the first three, related to being, choosing, and doing. They form the foundation of the therapist's belief system.

Faith Assumptions in Family Therapy

Carl Whitaker comments on his beliefs being central to his work as a family therapist in *Dancing with the Family*, p. 36:

> "Let me share with you some of my assumptions and biases as a way of conveying something personal about my work with families. This 'belief system,' as I've come to call it, lies at the core of any therapist's work."

He expands on the therapist's belief system in *The Evolution of Psychotherapy*, Jeffrey Zeig, ed., p. 82-3:

> "His belief system consists of the *known components*, those things which he's aware of, the *knowable components*, those things which he has become aware of with experience and evaluation, and the *unknowable*, those parts of the belief system which are beyond intellectual understanding. Secondary factors in his personhood and his belief system are the rational component (either intellectual and technical or political) and the irrational (those components that are a covert part of his experience, his evaluation and his symbolization of that experience)."

Summary

The three fundamentals beliefs already identified, the value of being, the necessity of choosing, and the inevitability of going one's own way, could be stated in a number of equally valid ways.

But however they are stated, they are seen as not subject to cancellation without major distress. They span an individual's development from birth through adolescence, reflecting and coordinating with physiological growth.

They are the bedrock of what is presented here, and what follows depends on them, even though they are still assumptions, capable of scientific illustration and demonstration, but not scientific proof.

Furthermore, these three fundamentals are assumed to exist before they are described. They are understood as given, in the same way that bones in our bodies are a given reality before any comment is made about their existence.

The four later developmental learnings are built on the foundation of the first three fundamental beliefs, and form an integrated whole.

The other fifteen assumptions are abstract concepts that support the seven developmental, experiential learnings. They do not evolve from physiological growth or from psychosocial crises, but are operational concepts that facilitate the application of the first seven learnings.

This approach leads to thinking of evolution on one's of faith as a series of "decisions" to believe in certain values and ideas as most useful for living.

These may not be self-conscious decisions which we are aware of making, but may be choices incorporated from others (parents, teachers or friends) without self-conscious intention or awareness. Sometimes we "do as the Romans do" in order to fit in, without consciously choosing to do so.

The process of learning to believe some values is inevitable, if we are to function effectively in the world. But what those values are, the *content* of the faith, is not inevitable, and can be revised from time to time. Our faith can grow and become more mature and more sophisticated as we grow and learn. Our emotional growth and learning occurs in many ways throughout our lives. Part of the learning process can occur in counseling and psychotherapy.

2) FAITH THAT THESE VALUES NOURISH HUMAN STRENGTH

We move toward what nourishes us, and away from the noxious. We desire to have more of what we perceive as loving and affirming, and to have less of what we see as harmful and destructive.

One implication of believing in the values described here is that they nourish human strength, nourish the human abilities to create a better life for the individual, family, community and world.

This point is emphasized by Howard Clinebell writing about the fulfillment of a spiritual need on p. 31 of *Well Being:*

> "*All of us need to have values, priorities, and life commitments centered in integrity, justice, and love, to guide us into personally and socially responsible living.* . . . Your values are guideposts on the road of your life that are essential to making countless decisions each day."

Values and Emotional Strength

Another therapist who saw and believed in the importance of the relationship of the individual with the human community is the psychoanalyst, Eric Erikson. In his book, *Insight and Responsibility,* he expressed the view that human emotional strength is rooted in developmental growth. He correlated particular virtues, or strengths, with the establishment of values that grow out of successful emotional development, calling them "psychological strengths."

Values are Developmentally Based

Erikson may have also been ahead of his time in emphasizing the importance of the cultural, trans-generational view of emotional growth and the values that support it:

> "Human strength, then, depends on a total process which regulates at the same time the *sequence of generations* and the *structure of society*" (p. 152).

The strengths Erikson describes grow out of and are established by the individual's successful negotiation of developmental crises that roughly correspond to what is described here as the three fundamental assumptions and the four other less fundamental assumptions, supported by the society.

He uses the word "virtue" to represent human strength as it develops throughout the human life cycle and is imparted from generation to generation. He summarizes his view on the development of virtue on p. 115 of Insight and Responsibility:

> "I will, therefore, speak of *Hope, Will, Purpose, and Competence* as the rudiments of virtue developed in childhood; of *Fidelity* as the adolescent virtue; and of *Love, Care, and Wisdom* as the central virtues of adulthood. In all their seeming discontinuity, these qualities depend on each other. Will cannot be trained until hope is secure, nor can love become reciprocal until fidelity has proven reliable.
>
> Also, each virtue and its place in the schedule of virtues is vitally interrelated to other segments

> of human development, such as the stages of psychosexuality which are so thoroughly explored in the whole of psychoanalytic literature, the psychosocial crises, and the steps of cognitive maturation."

He might be mistaken for a contemporary systems theorist, except that his choice of words suggests his psychoanalytic training.

But the point here is to illustrate the article of faith that when persons are nurtured in their emotional and psychological development, they will have the capacity to contribute positively to the cycle of generations. Such fully functioning individuals are needed to maintain the historical context for positive human development. This is another article of faith.

The Organic Plus Something More

When Erikson's book was published in 1964, it was not fashionable to speak in the same breath of faith and values and psychotherapy. Faith was associated with religious organizations and religion had a bad reputation with the psychoanalytic community.

But now, with persons like Candace Pert, neuropeptide researcher, speaking of "something more" than the organic viability of the individual leaving the body at the time of death, there is more respectability to speaking of the spiritual. To give the name "spirit" to this "something more" leaving the body is similar to saying that we don't know what else leaves the body at death, but that there is more to human life than the organic.

Two More Operational Assumptions

Two additional operational assumptions made here seem worth mentioning, since they shape our view of people and the way we treat them. They are both faith assumptions, and neither can be proven.

The first is that there is only one reality with which we deal, even though we do not fully understand it. A debate goes on in philosophical circles whether this is true. Here, we take the position operationally that an objective reality exists, even though we cannot fully comprehend it.

The second operational assumption is that the person is more than the sum of features that can be listed describing the person. The "person inside" is the author of what we experience when we encounter someone. The person is assumed to be the owner of or the creator of the characteristics we can see, hear, and touch. That "person inside" can be thought of as the soul or spirit of that individual.

The spirit to whom those characteristics belong is the person with whom we communicate. This idea will not find universal acceptance, but it is part of what is presented here.

3) FAITH IN ONE OBJECTIVE REALITY

Faith in one objective reality can be thought of theologically as well as scientifically. Theologically, we can refer to the other part of Nels Ferré's definition of religion. As stated before, he describes **religion** as our commitment to what we consider to be most high and most real (allowing for the limitations and distortions built into our humanity).

He then goes on to describe ***right religion*** as our commitment to what ***is*** most high and most real (about which we may grow into a more accurate understanding).

So there we are, stuck with our limited point of view, only approximating, but never fully arriving at a view of what ***is*** most high and most real. Ferré makes the assumption that God, the most High and most Real, does exist as an objective reality.

Objective Reality in Science

Scientists also make the assumption that there is one objective reality they are continuously striving to describe and understand more fully. Whether the study is of sub-atomic particles or the nature of Venus, the goal is first to see what is there, to describe the reality as accurately as possible.

Based on descriptive information, further study can reveal additional relationships and meanings. In physics, for example, the question is posed whether light is a particle or a wave. Of course, it is both, but we cannot **yet** describe fully how the two perspectives are related. Our faith is based on the assumption that objective reality does not change, but that our more accurate perception of it does change, and that an increasingly accurate description of it can be accomplished.

Objective Reality in Psychotherapy

Psychotherapy is not a science in the same way as sub-atomic physics is a science. However, therapists share the same assumption that there is an objective reality about human beings, and as we learn more, we will be able to achieve our goals more effectively.

Some argue the philosophical point of view that the only reality is our own perception, that varies from person to person. This is, of course, correct, since we have no way to know anything except through our own sensory apparatus, even when extended by technical means, such as telescopes, cameras, computers, and particle accelerators.

This point of view serves to underline the importance of **how** we understand each other and the world around us, since our perception is all we have. But it is our perception of something, whether that something "exists" or not. As a practical matter, we function as if other people do exist and that operational assumption becomes an article of faith.

As therapists we attempt to understand the reality of how people grow, function, get into emotional difficulty, and get out of emotional difficulty. We know our attempts at understanding are destined to be approximations, since we are not the creators of the universe, simply participants in the process, viewing it from a limited point of view by interpreting our perceptions.

It is important to avoid the "original sin" of believing we can eat the apple of knowledge and become as wise as God. We will never know all about reality, either as scientists or as theologians. We do well to accept that reality and our very limited though important role of understanding what we can and use our knowledge in the most constructive way we can.

4) FAITH IN THE SPIRIT WITHIN EACH PERSON

When I sat down with the very first class of my residency in psychotherapy, I was looking forward to what the instructor, Dr. Herbert Holt, an existential analyst, would present. We were all shocked when he began the class, not with small talk, but with the question, "Ladies and gentlemen, are you your excrement?"

Clearly taken aback, we stammered and groped for words to respond, not knowing the implication of his question, and also not wanting to say the wrong thing. Only later in the discussion did we understand that he was teaching us that a person is always more than his or her products, creations, words, thoughts, feelings, or body. He or she is the creator, not the product.

The person is the author of all that and more, and is never known directly, but only through those representations. That I remember his point many years later illustrates the effectiveness of his teaching method.

The Unknowable in Every Person

There is a mystery in the psyche of each person that is larger than the physical, the observable, the knowable. It centers on the difficulty of ever totally knowing oneself or others. We know how people look (their bodies), what they think (our perception of their communications), what they feel (an estimate based on what they express), and what they create (writings, widgets, children, etc.), without *fully* knowing the person behind the creation.

We never fully know this spiritual dimension of ourselves or others, and as a result, a mystery remains in all of us. Yet, each of us has a creator-self, by which we connect to that same spirit in others and in creation.

The mystery-surrounded person is the creator of some of what we can know, and perhaps is one way we participate in the larger creation. We seem to have been made very finite creators who can never be known except through our creations. Perhaps some people, psychics, saints, or poets, have the ability to directly contact their own inner selves or the psyche of others, but most of us are more limited in our experience.

Creativity and the Spiritual Dimension

In this context, we can think of our participation in the spiritual dimension as coming through our creator-self, greater than any "thing" we have to offer. Our self, our soul, our spirit is the source of what we offer, one step removed from the offering. The source is implied, but never directly revealed.

This participation in the spiritual dimension is present in the psychotherapeutic process, though we may not speak of it with our clients. It is the creator-self in the client to whom the therapist communicates, inviting and sometimes evoking positive change. When and how the client grows and changes is unpredictable, even though we create explanations in retrospect, in order to learn what is useful or not.

It is the creator-self in the therapist that enables the understanding and clarity necessary for loving treatment of the client, transcending theory systems and standardized technical interventions.

Extra-sensory Experiences

Another aspect of that mystery is our ability to be related to others beyond the limits of time and space. Such experiences may be described by those who experience them as being a kind of "connectedness," with the use of words like empathy, love, and oneness.

I experienced this connectedness on one occasion when I was newly married, and had the visual image of my wife having been in a minor traffic accident, in which she was bumped by a taxi while turning left at an intersection.

Some fifteen minutes later she called me and described the accident, just as I had visualized the whole event. I was not surprised, because I somewhat expected that she would call and tell me about it in the way she did. Since then, others have told me their own stories of a similar nature, and I accepted them as true in some way that I did not understand, and beyond my ability to explain. Now we know somewhat more about this phenomenon from experiments in physics.

Nonlocal Events

Physicists call the existence of information everywhere at once a *nonlocal* quality. The idea evolved from the work of the physicist John Stewart Bell, who in 1964 showed that once objects have been in contact with each other, a change in one causes immediate change in the other, no matter how distant they are from each other, based on actual experiments.

Larry Dossey uses this concept to describe the spiritual dimension of consciousness in his book, *Healing Words* (p. 84):

> "In my book *Recovering the Soul,* I discussed evidence from a wide variety of sources, including everyday experiences, suggesting that consciousness is non-local. This picture of the mind is quite different from that given in contemporary biology and medicine, which says that the mind is limited to the brain and to the present, and that it will perish when the body dies. . . .The nonlocal view suggests that thc mind cannot be limited to specific points in space (brains or bodies) or in time (the present moment), but is infinite in space and time; thus the mind is omnipresent, eternal, and immortal. If minds are indeed nonlocal, this means that in principle they cannot be walled off and separated from one another: at some level they are unitary and one."

Separate and Connected Go Together

When we listen to others they teach us who they are by what they say and do, even though we never know them fully. Our separateness is a position from which to contact others, to affirm a connectedness and an intimacy with all people and things that has been built into creation. Both our separateness and our connection to others call upon and enrich the spirit within us.

To whatever degrcc we experience a connection to all other beings, it affects our work as therapists, just as it affects all of our relationships with others. Let us explore in the next few pages some ways of understanding more about the spiritual dimension in which we participate.

5) THE SPIRITUAL DIMENSION OF LIFE

One difficulty in discussing the spiritual dimension of life is that of finding a clear consensus on its meaning. Yet, common threads emerge from the different points of view.

Definitions of the Spiritual Dimension

For example, Paul Gibson, writing in *The Family Journal*, quotes various authors who reflect certain themes describing spirituality as ". . . interconnectedness across time and space . . . horizon of our being . . . the core principle of conscious life . . . a unifying force which integrates all other dimensions . . . that spirituality involves feelings, a bodily sense, not simply a cognitive system . . . spiritual experiences lead to growth" (p. 47).

A conference on "Spirituality and Healing in Medicine" was held in 1995, sponsored by Harvard Medical School's Department of Continuing Education. While there were differences in understanding of spirituality, certain themes emerged. These same themes continue to be present in following yearly conferences.

Elizabeth Massey, writing in the *Journal of Pastoral Care*, stated that at the conference "definitions of spirituality which provide common ground between scientists and believers were 1) the experience of a transcendent divine in human life; and 2) the presence of a transcendent, transforming power which gives meaning and purpose to life and is usually referred to as 'God'" (p. 235).

Another difficulty in describing the spiritual dimension of life is that we can never fully have the viewpoint of the transcendent divine. We can only point, in a crudely formulated way, toward the transcendent power that breathes life into all things and enables growth and evolution to occur.

For our purposes, we will think of spirituality as a dimension of reality in which we participate through our inner connection to that reality. Our individual spirituality is enhanced to the degree that we succeed in aligning ourselves with the life-giving spiritual dimension that transcends all of us.

Acceptance

One guiding principle to help us in achieving alignment with the spiritual reality of the universe is that we connect with the spiritual dimension by acceptance of all creation, and the affirmation of the harmony in it.

As we will use the word here, acceptance is the acknowledgment of what exists; that people, things, and nature are what they are, descriptively. The only "judgment" involved in acceptance is the attempt to be descriptively as accurate as possible. Acceptance includes the understanding of what we deem to be destructive and dysfunctional, that which some call evil.

Acceptance as used here has nothing to do with approval or disapproval, nothing to do with endorsement or condemnation. It has to do with understanding the inner nature of people and things and valuing that understanding. Acceptance has to do with using that understanding of the inner nature of people in whatever ways we choose, including our finding ways to minimize and cancel the evil we see.

Possibly the most effective way to minimize and cancel the evil we see is to cancel alienation from self and others, the recommendation made by Paul Tillich. To the degree that sin can be defined as alienation, acceptance is the loving antidote.

Affirmation

Affirmation, as used here, is validation of the logic of the other person's point of view, of the biologically natural process that occurs in growing things, and of the laws of physics. Affirmation is also validation of the reality of the pain and suffering that exists in the world, resulting from a rejection of the natural order and condemnation of the reality of others.

Acceptance and affirmation enable us to be more powerful in dealing with the world as-it-is because we are not focused on objecting and fighting the world as-it-is. Put another way, we do not attempt to play God.

Acceptance and affirmation can be described and understood as resulting in unconditional love. Such love is personal, calls upon our emotions, and connects us to the people around us. We can say that love connects us to others through the spiritual dimension of life.

Our Spiritual Connectedness

Since we are already connected to everyone spiritually, the process of meeting and becoming acquainted with another person is the process of becoming self-consciously aware of what already exists: the relationship with the other person.

The psychotherapist can think of the intake interview as an uncovering of his or her relationship with the client, as well as developing an understanding of the client's presenting problem.

This is not a static process, because what already exists is always evolving and changing, like the currents and tides of the sea. The key point is that the connection with others and all things already exists, just as the sea already exists before the movement of the tides.

We can also say that the spiritual dimension connects us to non-animal things. We can know of the spiritual dimension of life through our contact with the natural order of the universe. This contact is personal because the *meaning* of our relationships comes from within us, engaging our emotional responses.

This point was brought home to me in a personal way through the story a friend told me while hiking one Fall day. He described the way his six year old son, John, came in one day from playing outside, covered up and down his frontside with a sticky, sap-like substance.

His father noticed his sticky look, became somewhat curious, and so asked in a friendly manner, "Where have you been?" Without hesitation John responded eagerly, "I've been hugging trees!"

Of course, what could be more natural than to hug a tree? Carlos Castenada writes in some detail about our close spiritual connection to trees as well as the animal kingdom.

Spirituality and Harmony with Nature

The natural order of the universe includes the laws of physics, as with the vacuum above the curve of the airplane wing giving lift to move the airplane upward. The success of the airplane lies in it's cooperation with the natural order and it's inherent power. The natural order is also found in the way our genes define our bodies' growth, development and maintenance.

All of this can be understood as part of the spiritual dimension, the natural order of things. We can endeavor to align ourselves with this life-giving power, even though we do so more or less successfully.

The more we succeed in aligning ourselves with all the realities of the universe, the higher the level our spiritual functioning becomes. And as a corollary, our physical, emotional, and cognitive functioning is also raised to a higher level. In some mysterious way that is still unclear to most of us, the spiritual embraces and is a part of all reality and is available to all, both within and ourside organized religious groups.

The Vastness of the Spiritual Dimension

Our participation in the spiritual dimension is at once deeply personal and at the same time awesome, because of the vastness of the reality in which we participate. We may call the reality of the spiritual dimension God, with God's Spirit present in all creation. Others reject a concept of God and think of the spiritual in other terms. Whatever the symbols, they point to a personal, emotionally very significant spiritual connection with others and with creation as a whole.

The Spiritual Dimension is Holistic

Our participation in the spiritual dimension, while engaging our feelings, goes beyond our subjective experience of them to involve our body chemistry. A growing body of research in psycho-neuroimmunology makes clear that our immune response is directly affected by our emotional stance. Our feelings reflect what is emotionally important to us.

For example, research has been done by Doc Lew Childres at the Institute of HeartMath. He found that when, through a form of guided visualization, an individual moves into an emotional position of loving appreciation of life, he or she has a measurable decrease in cortisol levels, an increase in the saliva immune factor IGA, and an increase in the ability of white blood cells to carry oxygen. Love improves immune system functioning.

This holistic view of body/mind functioning involves not only cognitive reframing. It involves an emotional shift into loving appreciation of others that affects body chemistry in a positive way. From our perspective here it is a participation in and an alignment with the inherently affirming and loving spiritual dimension.

Spirituality is Interconnected

Here is another illustration of our participation in the spiritual dimension, found in an experiment directed by William G. Braud at the Mind Science Foundation in San Antonio, Texas, with statistically significant results. It measured the ability of one person's autonomic nervous system to influence another person in a different room. As reported by Sperry Andrews in the journal, *Alternative Therapies* 2(3) p.40:,

> "A one-way, closed-circuit video system allowed for the periodic observation of a volunteer by an experimenter. With this protocol, a series of volunteers were monitored for autonomic nervous system (electrodermal) reactions during both observation and non-observation (control) periods. The volunteers did not know when or for how long they were observed. Results remained undisclosed within automated computer memory until each stage of the study was complete. This series of tests indicated that the autonomic nervous system activity of one person is strongly correlated with the focused attention and intention of a conventionally isolated second person."

Andrews, convinced of a connection between all people and nature, founded the Human Connection

Project, designed to conduct a long term study linking five brain research laboratories in North America.

They will be electronically linked so as to measure EEG, EKG, galvanic skin response, plethysmography, and breathing response of geographically isolated participants, in relation to each other.

They are testing the hypothesis that a connectedness among individuals exists that will evoke a group consciousness, similar to the way individual cells function as part of an individual's consciousness.

Within the frame of reference used here, this study could be described as an experiment in intentional spirituality that has the potential to raise our participation in the reality of interpersonal connectedness to a new level of integration and loving good will.

In his article, "Promoting a Sense of Connectedness Among Individuals by Scientifically Demonstrating the Existence of a Planetary Consciousness" (*Alternative Therapies in Health and Medicine, pp. 39-45),* Andrews summarizes:

> "The subjective experience of feeling consciously connected with others and our environment--to that which is larger than ourselves--has been found to promote physical and mental health, or well-being. Various ways of evaluating this sense of connectedness have been studied under controlled scientific conditions. Through these studies, more has been learned about the effect of connectedness, ways of facilitating a sense of connection, and how to approach some objective understanding of its physical basis and human value. Evidently, we do share a interconnected rapport with others and with nature."

Unseen Forces in the Universe

It is difficult to conceive of a force, an energy, a spiritual connection between people and things, because we cannot *see* the energy or the connection in a measurable way. There is an interesting parallel in quantum mechanics, related to the most basic, irreducible particle in creation, called the "quark."

The current scientific understanding is that the quark is the basic particle of which everything is made. The quark has been experimentally identified and measured in physics laboratories. Stephen Hawking, in his 1988 book, *A Brief History of Time*, describes a number of principles currently in use by modern physicists. He summarizes, "Matter on earth is made up mainly of protons and neutrons, which in turn are made up of quarks. . . . We have evidence from cosmic rays that the same is true for all the matter in our galaxy." (p. 76)

These particles have an effect upon each other by emitting "force-carrying" particles. He explains:

> "What happens is, that a matter particle, such as an electron or a quark, emits a force-carrying particle. The recoil from this emission changes the velocity of the matter particle. The force-carrying particle then collides with another matter particle and is absorbed. This collision changes the velocity of the second particle, just as if there had been a force between the two matter particles (pp. 68 & 69)."

Even more startling is the invisibility of the force-carrying particles, which are called "virtual" particles, rather than real particles.

> "The force-carrying particles exchanged between matter particles are said to be virtual

particles because, unlike 'real' particles, they cannot be directly detected by a particle detector. We know they exist, however, because they do have a measurable effect: They give rise to forces between matter particles." (pp. 68-69)

One of the four identified forces is the gravitational force. The virtual particles, gravitons, are exchanged between the real particles making up the sun and the earth, creating gravitational energy. "Although the exchanged particles are virtual [and thus unable to be detected directly], they certainly do have a measurable effect--they make the earth orbit the sun." (p. 70) (The other three forces are the electromagnetic force, the strong nuclear force, and the weak nuclear force).

Nonlocal Events

From this cosmic, quantum mechanics perspective it is not so difficult to conceive of forces between the particles that make up humans and other living things. If these forces between particles do exist, and if the nonlocal effect is a reality of the physical world, then the therapeutic relationship could conceivably extend beyond the clinical hour spent in the therapist's office.

The gestalt of the therapist toward the client and the gestalt of the client toward the therapist is an ongoing reality, especially when one person is consciously focused upon the other. When the two persons are focused on each other, their geographical proximity may become less significant.

The nonlocal character of communication also seems to be found between pets and their owners. Larry Dossey, M.D., recounts the story of a dog that found it's owner in a place it had never been before (*Alternative Therapies in Health and Medicine. 1996;2(3)).*

He gives the example of "Bobbie, a collie who was traveling with a family from Ohio to their new home in Oregon, where Bobbie had never been. During a stop in Indiana, Bobbie got lost. After a diligent attempt to find her, the family finally gave up and proceeded westward. Months later, Bobbie appeared at the new home in Oregon. This was not a look-alike animal: she still had her name tag and several identifying marks and scars."

In addition, there are telesomatic events, in which what is being experienced by one person is communicated to and perceived by someone emotionally close to that person. Dossey goes on to describe several examples, one of which is that of a woman who "suddenly doubled over, clutching her chest as if in severe pain, and said, 'Something has happened to Nell, she has been hurt.' Two hours later the sheriff came, stating that Nell had died on the way to the hospital. She had been involved in an auto accident, in which a piece of the steering wheel had penetrated her chest."

Dossey believes that "telesomatic events are nonlocal expressions of consciousness. They demonstrate the ability of love to reach out through space and time and unite us as one. They show that 'connectedness' and 'becoming one' are not just poetry or metaphor, but concrete reality. They reveal that, at some level of the whole person, unity -- not separation -- is fundamental."

The Aura Around Us

Less difficult to fathom is the effect of non-contact "therapeutic touch" healing, as pioneered by Dolores Krieger, Ph.D., of New York University. In this process, the hands of the healer are moved closely over the body of the person being healed to transfer healing energy. As a result the auras or electrical fields of both persons interact with each other.

It is fairly common knowledge that each person has an "aura" surrounding his or her body, that can be discerned by others trained to do so, by sight or by touch. An aura can be captured on a photographic film, the same medium used to identify particles in the physics laboratory. A large group of practitioners use therapeutic touch healing techniques.

We Are All Connected

So we return to the place where we began, that there is an experiential connection between people and things that can be understood as existing, even though we may not be able to see or identify it by ordinary means. The connection is not something that is good or bad, holy or evil. *It simply exists,* whether we like it or not.

Dossey concludes the introduction to his editorial as follows:

> "One of the greatest discoveries of our century--perhaps any century--may be the nonlocal connectedness that exists between the spectacular variety of entities that make up our universe. As we've seen, this connectedness is manifested between subatomic particles, mechanical systems, humans and machines, human and animals, and humans themselves. When this nonlocal bond operates between people, we call it 'love.' When it unites distant subatomic particles, what should we call this manifestation? Should we choose a safe, aseptic term such as 'nonlocally correlated behavior,' or bite the bullet and call it a rudimentary form of love? I am not suggesting that people and electrons experience love and empathy to the same degree; but we are free to wonder whether

> the unity of distant subatomic particles may be a primordial kind of empathy -- a proto-love -- that swells in intensity with increasing biological complexity, emerging fully formed as love and compassion in people."

The reality of this connection is what we refer to when speaking of the spiritual dimension of life, including our experience of it as intensely personal. Perhaps participation in the spiritual dimension is not so personal for the trees and water, the sun and the earth. But for humans, the spiritual is deeply emotional and personal, and this inevitably becomes part of the therapeutic process.

6) EXPERIENCING THE SPIRITUAL DIMENSION

We can become aware of the spiritual dimension of life through our senses as we soak in the beauty of a sunset, the smell of ocean spray, the warmth of an afternoon sun, or the delight of nourishing food. Our experience through our sensory nerve endings gives us an awareness of participating in a larger, non-sensory, spiritual dimension of life, beyond what we can imagine.

"I-Thou" Communication

More intensely, we may contact other persons directly at a point of mutual awareness and understanding that goes beyond words. This intimate contact of one soul touching another can be described as the "I-Thou" communication of which Martin Buber writes in his classic *I and Thou*.

As an experience of the spiritual dimension of life, some people will speak of the "I-Thou" experience in religious terms, as being in contact with God's presence, or Spirit. Whether spoken of in religious terms or not, such awareness of a connection with the unifying spirit of humanity can be thought of as nurturing the “sacred space” that exists between people through an acceptance and affirmation of others as they are.

We can think of a commitment to living in the spiritual dimension of life as a commitment to creating and maintaining that sacred space which is the relationship. We can either contaminate that space with trash or sanctify it with whatever is loving and healing.

Love and the Spiritual Are United

Participation in the spiritual dimension of life generates love that unconditionally accepts and affirms creation and everything in it. This appreciation of life includes a kind of awe that acknowledges the amazing wisdom and beauty built into creation.

Our best alternative is to accept and affirm the world as it is. We can love the world as it is, without taking the position that if only we were in control of everything we could make the world “the way it should be.” We have such difficulty in fully understanding the nature of things that it is grossly arrogant to think of “fixing” it. Yet, we know something of loving others, and can apply what we do know to make our own small contribution to sanctify the space within which we live.

One model for this acceptance and affirmation of life is demonstrated by the prayer of Jesus Christ while being crucified: “Father, forgive them, they do not know what they are doing.” (Philips, The New Testament, Luke 23:32) Jesus disapproved of their actions, but had love and forgiveness, not hatred in his heart.

Our Human Limitations

One experience of our human limitation is found in our inability to understand all the new discoveries in physics, which are so numerous no one but a specialist can keep up with a small corner of what is being studied.

The best we can do is accept our lack of comprehensive understanding of what creation is, to say nothing about why it is the way it is. As Stephen Hawking points out, when "time" is taken into account, God as creator is clearly beyond our comprehension:

> "It's a bit like the old paradox: Can God make a stone so heavy he can't lift it? But the idea that God might want to change his mind is an example of the fallacy, pointed out by St. Augustine, of imagining God a being existing in time: time is a property of the universe that God created. Presumably he knew what he intended when he set it up!" (p.98)

Limitations, Psychopathology, and Sin

It is possible to be in the world, to be alive, and have a very non-personal relationship to other people and things. It is also possible to have a limited or distorted personal relationship. As psychotherapists, one way we can describe these difficulties in relationships is as a symptom of emotional difficulty or immaturity, and find a DSM IV classification with which to label it.

We can see relationship difficulties theologically, as does Paul Tillich, a protestant philosophical theologian, who defines sin as "separation" from self and others. Evil can be thought of as an attempt to make alienation the value on which the spiritual dimension is based.

But however described, a lack of personal affirmation of creation diminishes one's spiritual depth and ultimately nurtures bitterness. The rebel who goes against reality loses, in the long run.

The Affirmation of Life

The alternative to rebellion against reality-as-it-is is the affirmation of life and the world as it is, the basis for participation in the spiritual dimension of life. In order to participate, just as in any area, the individual must be open to join the process. This is what makes the participation personal and genuine.

A person may describe a spiritual experience with words like, "God spoke to me." Or, someone may speak of a personal relationship with God. Or, participation in the spiritual dimension may reshape the meaning of a person's life and redefine the way he or she acts, feels, and behaves. That, too, is intensely personal.

When personal spirituality is defined as the individual and God having a speaking relationship, in which they literally talk over a cup of coffee as friends do, it is difficult for most people to fathom. Hearing God speak in the same way we hear the words a friend speaks to us is not what typically takes place.

When a person is in touch, personally, with the people and the world around him or her, new meanings or understandings may emerge out of those connections, much as a virtual particle has its effect on the matter particle it left and the matter particle that absorbs it. To make personal one's connections to the world is to participate in the spiritual dimension of life. Then in internally validated ways, we know the message that God is sending us. The word from God may come to us with certainty, though without auditory clarity.

How God Speaks to Us

This can be understood as the way God speaks to us, through our internal awareness of what is "most high and most real." The words describing our new understanding may pop into our thinking without effort, as an experience of God's spiritual presence in our life.

This contact with the essence of another person or of nature or of what we will do next provides us with a new and very concrete understanding of the meaning of our life. We may understand it as God's message to us or as our learning something of the mystery of creation.

When we accept the world as it is, including the pain and suffering, we affirm and participate in the spiritual dimension of creation by replacing estrangement with reconciliation. This does not imply an affirmation of or valuing of suffering.

On the contrary, accepting the world as it is clarifies suffering as an offense to the harmony in life which spirituality reflects and represents. Such acceptance puts us in a position to understand what we can do to relieve pain and suffering while understanding and appreciating its significance to those who bear it. Our commitment to purifying the space in which we live generates the energy to use our best efforts to do what is loving.

Three Meanings of Love

Accepting the world and the people in it is the first step in loving the world and the people in it. Accepting people as they are leads to affirmation of their value, the belief that each person is precious simply because of his or her existence. This belief is part of loving, and uncovers a spiritual connection with others because it affirms an essential element of human functioning.

We use "love" to mean several different things, according to the way and context in which the word is used. The three primary meanings of love the way it is commonly used are 1) enjoyment, 2) our treatment of others, and 3) our emotional involvement with others and things of importance to us.

The first meaning is evident in statements like, "I love vacations, when I can just relax and do the things I like most." Or, "I love bagels." Or, "I love being with you." Enjoyment is being highlighted and is the essential meaning in those contexts.

In the second usage of love, a parent might observe a son taking care of a pet, and say something like, "Look how he loves his cat," meaning that he is taking good care of the animal. Or, an observation might be made of a person who has forgiven another for an inconsiderate or hurtful action, "She is such a loving person." Love can be understood as treating others well, even though the loving person might not find the process pleasurable. And we are all aware of the love of a parent for a child that calls for loving treatment of the child even when the child is doing things that are offensive to the parent.

In the third instance, love may represent an emotional investment in another's life. This is the occasion for valuing the relationship because of the importance of shared experiences, or simply a commitment to care about the other person(s). For example, men who have been through battle experiences together may love each other in this particular way of being connected emotionally because of the shared traumatic experience, and meet from time to time to commemorate their experience.

Interestingly, couples may be very deeply emotionally invested in each other, even when they have not had a particularly enjoyable experience being married. They may have even treated each other in emotionally or physically abusive ways. But, having shared significant life experiences, they are emotionally related in a very significant way.

By living through various life circumstances, people develop a caring for each other, even though their relationship may not be characterized by significant pleasure based on treating each other well.

Love is not used in this book primarily as a symbol of enjoyment, though that is a common use of the word.

The focus on love here is in the dual sense of 1) making a positive emotional investment in others and the world, and as a result, 2) treating others in positive ways. This is another way of describing the emotional connection to all of creation that puts one in the spiritual dimension. The spiritual dimension is inherently a loving dimension, making it a very personal experience.

Love and Childhood (and Adult) Wounds

We all have childhood wounds that carry over to some degree into the present, causing difficulties in everyday living and relationships. One way to think about these wounds is that we were not loved -- treated positively -- in ways that we needed to be adequately nurtured in our emotional growth. As a result, we may come to conclusions about ourselves, about others, and about ways to avoid being hurt in the future that create the very pain we wish to avoid.

The other possibility is that though we were loved, we were unable to take in the warmth and nurture and use it for our own growth, to some degree.

In either case, we did not embrace the self-acceptance we needed to cancel alienation from self and others. What was lacking in love can be thought of, in developmental terms, as a deficit of a particular kind of loving treatment, or an inability to take in and accept loving treatment, at a particular period in our lives.

Valuing Oneself and Others

People unsure of their value as persons or who doubt their validity as separate human beings may want reassurance they are loved, nurtured, and cared for, and that they are valued by others, by God and the universe.

They want the inner knowledge and certainty that they are important simply because they exist, the first fundamental psychological learning about life.

When a child does not absorb this understanding as an infant and small child, he or she suffers emotionally, and will be motivated to deal with that pain as an adult, perhaps in therapy. With commitment to emotional work, an adult can learn to value himself or herself in a way that may not have been established as a child.

That learning is the same as accepting and incorporating the fundamental faith assumption that each person has infinite worth, symbolized in the belief that God loves all people unconditionally. Valuing oneself is fundamental to the spiritual dimension of life, forming the foundation for valuing all life and creation.

Making One's Own Decisions

When love is given to others, it can be understood as "accepting and affirming others as they are." Looking at later emotional development, loving can be seen as an affirmation of others' gene-driven exercise of autonomy over themselves. Autonomy and independence does not lead to isolation from others. It leads to relationships built on the foundation of intentional choices. Belief in the "built in," essential nature of autonomy is another gift of love, creating spiritual connections with others.

The truly autonomous individual doesn't need to fight to achieve what he or she has already accomplished, a clear awareness that each person decides for himself or herself.

Autonomy is the prerequisite for choosing God's way, to accept creation as it is, a choice freely made, with no coercion at all. A person struggling to establish this principle will need reassurance that autonomy is mandated by the nature of mankind, so each person can freely choose to affirm and love the world as it is.

It might seem strange to describe affirmation of autonomy as part of the spiritual dimension of life, since much theological thinking assumes that individual independence is the same as disobedience to God's will. However, clarity about one's own independence is part of the foundation upon which a decision to commit oneself to God or anything else is made. Genuine autonomy makes faith unshakable.

Charting One's Own Direction

A similar process occurs with the exhortation to give one's life over to the control of God, to the control of a twelve step program, or to the control of anything else.

When a person is developmentally not ready to exercise autonomous decisions over his or her own life, it may be a life-saving and life-giving decision to surrender control to a benevolent authority, in much the same way that a child depends upon his or her parents for guidance. Alcoholics Anonymous and other similar programs have proven their tremendous, life-saving value in this regard.

Making My Way God's Way -- Cooperation

Developmentally, however, the most positive emotional and spiritual goal is growth of personal initiative to manage and guide one's own life in the most positive directions, a step beyond blind obedience. This involves the exercise of personal autonomy to move toward cooperation with the structure of the universe.

At times, theologians and others have seen this period of personal initiative in emotional development as setting up a duality of "My way versus God's way," with the solution being submission to God's authority. This might seem to mean the giving up of any active role in decision making, and the adoption of a passive position of obedience to an authority.

But the essential point can be made by saying that a person may be committed to matching his or her way to God's way, insofar as the person's growing understanding of God's way will allow. This way of putting it implies an active role in searching out one's best understanding of God's way, the way of creation, and a desire and willingness to follow it.

In this context, encouraging acceptance of the world as God created it moves beyond the duality of "My way versus God's way," with the solution being a free choice of God's way, as well as we can know it. Understood this way, "My way becomes God's way, by my choice."

Success in this developmental task can be described as accepting the world as it is, corresponding to Erik Erikson's description of the primary emotional task of adolescence as being learning to choose the inevitable.

Thinking in terms of "my way" in opposition to "the way things are" discourages the exercise of individual initiative (except in the case of competitive situations, such as sports or war), and goes against creativity and innovation. Experimentation with one's own way to be and do things is a step along the journey of establishing self-direction in the face of the childish need to do (or fight) what is desired by a caretaker in order to survive. A person succeeds (and is connected to the spiritual dimension of life) when he or she cooperates with the way things are, so that “my way” becomes the way of the universe, the way of God.

Accepting Others As They Are

Accepting people as they are leads to affirmation of the different ways people look, think, talk, and behave. Affirmation of differences is not *endorsement* of all ideas and behavior. It is the acceptance of people as they are as a basis for defining how to relate. It is a position of loving treatment of others, affirming the richness of the contributions each can make *because* of the differences from the other we each have.

Much time is spent in marriage counseling and other therapeutic sessions dealing with conflict over differences people have with each other. Learning how to listen to, understand, and empathize with others *as they are* is a major task for many clients.

Affirmation of and acceptance of the differences among people is another loving thread of spiritual connection to others, since it affirms another essential of human nature that we all share.

"And the Greatest of These is Love"

Love is tied to the spiritual dimension of life because loving, the way it is used here, is an emotional investment in caring about someone or something. To love is also to treat others well, consider them important, and open the door to enjoying them as well.

Such loving is the love described in most world religions, understood as essential to the nurturing of children as they grow into the unique person that each becomes. Couples who are deeply spiritual and loving create a sacred space within which their children can grow and experience affirmation in their own lives. This richness can be passed on to others to make the world in which we live a safer and more loving place to be.

With respect to the spiritual dimension of life, love is integral, because it expresses acceptance and affirmation of all creation. By assuming the existence of the spiritual dimension of reality, the connectedness of all things, life becomes an adventure of discovery of that reality in all its forms. Psychotherapy can be one way to get back on the positive track of that adventuresome journey into loving life.

7) SUMMARY: A WAY TO RELATE VALUES, FAITH, AND PSYCHOTHERAPY

The theoretical assumptions discussed so far have implications for the clinical practice of psychotherapy, as well as for living in general. People who seek therapy are concerned to improve the quality of their everyday living, either to relieve their pain, or to enhance their ability to do well according to their own values.

It may be helpful to summarize the discussion up to this point as a prelude to viewing the implications of values for therapeutic technique.

1) Psychotherapy is a means of helping people improve their lives, according to their own goals.
2) In describing what is helpful to people, we make assumptions about human nature, that are, functionally, articles of faith. Some of them are scientifically provable, some are not. Operating assumptions are articles of faith because they are values embraced by the believer, not because the believer is part of an organized religious tradition.

3) Psychotherapists, as well as others, are emotionally invested in living out those principles, since they must have some values on which to base their lives and their professional work. By being aware of values they can respect the right of others to differ.

4) The three most fundamental articles of faith to be affirmed are that:

   1. People have value because they exist.
   2. People make decisions for and are in control of themselves.
   3. People think, feel, and act in their own way.

5) Four other, less fundamental articles of faith can support the importance of people to:

   1. Affirm their own sexuality.
   2. Become economically independent/responsible.
   3. Develop their creativity.
   4. Share their wisdom and resources with others who have an interest.

6) Fifteen other faith assumptions basic to psychotherapy shape what we communicate to clients. They are that:

   1. There is a difference between thinking/feeling.
   2. There is a difference between feeling/behavior.
   3. Emotions provide power to act.
   4. Thinking gives us the ability to solve problems.
   5. Human nature is an organic whole.
   6. Condemnation of self or others is destructive.
   7. People learn from experience.
   8. Human beings are social animals.
   9. We always select what we say or do.
   10. We are always doing something.

11. What we do affects others.
12. We use values as criteria for action.
13. It is desirable to be aware of our beliefs.
14. Symptoms are solutions.
15. No theory or technique is ultimate.

7) These values are articles of faith that grow out of the successful negotiation of the tasks that physiological growth and the social environment hand us.

They are beliefs we cannot prove. Some such set of beliefs, such as the ones listed above, are believed and taught by the therapist, intentionally or not. The client also adheres to some set of beliefs. The therapist will have an emotional investment in his or her beliefs that will influence the course of therapy. It is better to be aware of what they are, in order to be clear about what articles of faith one may be promoting.

8) How we understand the identity of a person is significant. A person can be understood as being the creator of his or her ideas, feelings, and behavior, but is not completely defined by them. This person-as-creator lives in and cares for a physical body, but is not totally defined by that, either. These products or characteristics of a person are important, but are one step removed from the person who creates or owns them. We do not experience the essence of people directly, but only through what they present to us.

9) The spiritual dimension of life is our personally meaningful connection to other people and things, based on our acceptance and affirmation of the world and all that is in it. The spiritual dimension affirms principles of being, choosing, and doing as part of the psychological reality of humanity. Our spirituality represents our involvement in a life-force that exists on its own, requiring love as the means of participation.

CHAPTER V
APPLICATION OF VALUES AND FAITH TO THERAPEUTIC TECHNIQUE

Up to this point, we have discussed the operational assumptions made by therapists that comprise a central set of values. Those values may be expressed in a variety of theoretical systems, and may be implemented with a variety of therapeutic techniques. In this chapter, we will explore the ways these values or faith assumptions can shape techniques, the therapeutic interventions used by the therapist.

When working with clients, the psychotherapist must do *something,* select what to say, what to do, how to sit, whether to be on time, end on time, what fee to charge, and so on. All these inevitable decisions reflect the therapist's way of working and communicate to the client a point of view about the client, people, and the world in general. These communications are an expression of his or her therapeutic style.

The therapist's therapeutic style is also shaped by values held by the therapist about his or her self-worth, autonomy, and ways of working. The way the therapist treats the client will be an indirect reflection of his or her own value system.

A Clinical Example of Values

Following is a therapy session that illustrates the clinical application of some of the values and beliefs that have been described up to this point. After this example, we will go on to discuss how each of the fundamental assumptions and values discussed in the first half of the book have been applied in their therapeutic work by various well-known therapists.

This session with Don and Nancy (not their real names) illustrates the way beliefs on the part of the therapist and the part of the clients affect their view of themselves and what to do to succeed in life. At times, the methods Nancy used to take care of herself created more of the same pain she was trying to avoid.

Nancy had called me before this fifth session to say that Don was complaining that the counseling sessions were not addressing their problems directly enough, and that he didn't want to come back. She then said they might as well get a divorce because they had been to marriage counseling twice before and this seemed to her just like his previous refusal to go back to further therapy sessions. So he relented, and told her he would keep the appointment after all.

Following is a version of the session, written immediately after it ended. Since it was written from memory, it is shorter than a tape transcript, but captures the essence of the process. The notes in parentheses describe my view of the process, and indicate the procedures, beliefs and values I hoped to implement at the time.

Therapist: Let's take some time now to assess where you are and how you're doing in the process of therapy. (I wanted Nancy to know that I had taken seriously her concern about which she had telephoned me. I wouldn't follow the Imago Relationship Therapy process as we had been doing in previous sessions, but instead work in a modified way this session).

Therapist: How did it go with the agreement about keeping the dog off the couch? (This is a reference to an agreement from last session that Nancy would keep the dog off the couch, as an unconditional gift to Don. My question was also meant to express my view of them as two separate people who were able to make a mutually satisfying agreement and keep it).

Nancy: Oh, that went very well.

Don: Yeah, just fine. That's working out well. But that's a minor problem. That's the reason I used that issue at the time, because it's easy to solve.

Th: Other things bother you more. (What you have to say is important, and I will not criticize you).

Don: (To Nancy) You can say what you want to talk about.

Nancy: No, you can talk.

Don: No, no. Go ahead.

Nancy: Well, Don thinks I tell him what to do, and that I'm too critical of him . . .

Th: (gently) Do you usually speak for Don? (I asked this provocative question for two reasons. One was to use the response in a differential diagnostic sense, to see how "separate" they were. The second reason was to confront them with the reality of their separateness).

Nancy: No, I usually don't. He just wanted me to start. I don't ever talk for him.

Don: It's just that she is so critical of me. And even in public, when we're out with friends, she'll say something like, "He's terrible," after someone says "He's really good at that." She's always been like that.

Nancy: I have always been like that. I just say what's on my mind, whatever it is.

Th: Do you agree with Don, that you are critical, and say derogatory things about him even when other people are around? (Here my goal is to support the validity of their having different points of view, even when they agree, and to be totally sure that she takes responsibility for acting the way Don had described).

Nancy: Yes, I do.

Th: When you say those critical things, what are you feeling? (Here I am establishing the difference between thinking and feeling, as well as moving toward the emotional power connected to feelings).

Nancy: I feel angry.

Don: Yeah, she's angry.

Th: Where in your body do you sense the feeling? (My assumption here is that human nature is an organic whole, and that there is a difference between feelings and physical action).

Nancy: Right here, in my chest (points to her sternum).

Th: So you are aware of what you are feeling, and how you experience it in your body, perhaps even before you say anything. (I intend to clarify by separating thinking, feeling, and behavior).

Nancy: I always know what I am feeling, and before I say anything about Don, I know I feel angry.

Th: When we are angry, we want something we don't have, or we're getting something we don't want, which is the same thing. So, when you're angry, Nancy, there is something you want. (I teach about interpreting anger in a way that turns it into a problem-solving challenge. I also imply that thinking gives us the ability to solve problems and that emotions give us the energy to act).

Nancy: I want Don to listen to me and not ignore me. He treats me like I don't matter to him.

Don: I don't ignore you. I just can't always give you my undivided attention. Can't you just wait until later to talk to me about whatever it is when we're home alone? When you call and I'm in the middle of something at work, I can't always just drop it and talk with you.

Nancy: No, because I have to deal with things at the time, I can't wait until later.

Don: But you can't always get what you want at the moment. Sometimes you have to put things off until later. I don't always get what I want at the time, but I know I can come back to it later.

Nancy: I can't stand to wait until later.

Th: What does waiting until later mean to you? (I imply that it is desirable to be aware of our values and beliefs, and support the principle that she can think in her own way, different from what Don is saying).

Nancy: That I'm unimportant and what I have to say is unimportant (tears).

Th: (With empathy) I can see, when you think you are unimportant, how difficult and painful it would be to put off until later what you want to say. (I am communicating that symptoms are solutions to painful problems, and also validate the reality of her painful position and her way of dealing with it).

Nancy: Yes, I just can't wait.

Th: How did you learn that waiting until later means you are not important? (This comment supports the belief that we all learn from experience).

Nancy: I never could wait. Just like my mother. The strange part is, that when we're together, that's the way we talk to each other, just say whatever is on our mind, and we get along fine.

Th: You play by the same rules. (Here I intend to note that we each are ultimately responsible for selecting what we believe and how we act.).

Nancy: Yes.

Th: So you learned how to say what is on your mind when you were growing up, following your mother's example. (This comment relates to learning from experience and the reality that we are social animals and accommodate to our social reality in order to maintain emotional contact).

Nancy: Yeah, because if I didn't speak up, I didn't get listened to. I wasn't important in the family. . . . (tears) . . . I learned to deal with things at the time because if I didn't deal with it then, I'd never be listened to. I wasn't important . . . (tears).

Th: I can see how painful it was to you not be listened to, because every child needs to know she is important and that what she has to say is important. That must have been very painful for you, believing you didn't count. (This is an empathic validation of the first psychological fundamental, that she has value because she exists. I also meant it as a validation of the third psychological fundamental, that every child needs to know her way is valued as "good enough" by her parents. I thought she was less clear about the third fundamental, but I couched my comment in the words of the first fundamental, so as to cover both simultaneously).

Nancy: It was. And my father was never home, and didn't have any time for me at all. So I couldn't count on him for anything. He didn't want to be bothered by me.

Don: I want you to know that you're important to me, even though I can't always drop everything, like when you call at work and I'm in the middle of something. I care about you and maybe you could think about all the good times we've had and if for the moment things are not going well, we know things will be better and maybe even better than before.

Nancy: I don't understand at all where he's coming from. I just can't understand.

Th: Well, let's see if you can at least understand what he said. Will you mirror what he just said, "I hear you saying . . . " (My moving in this direction is based on the assumption that "the truth will make you free." Put in other, syllogistic terms, "Let's see if you will accept what Don says as important enough for you to listen to, even if it contradicts your assumptions about him and you").

Nancy: I hear you saying that I should remember the good times, and think about how things will be better. Do I have it?"

Don: No, not at all. I said that I love you and that I will always love you and that you're important to me, and that just because I don't take time to pay attention to you at a particular time, it doesn't mean that you're not important to me. And that you can remember our good times and know that we can have more good times in the future.

Th: (to Nancy) Do you believe him? (I assume the value of being clear about and owning our own beliefs).

Nancy: No. I think he's pretending.

Th: You know him pretty well. And my guess is that you can usually tell when someone is not telling the truth. Is that correct? (I am affirming that she can know what she knows about Don, and use it in a constructive way).

Nancy: Yes, I can tell.

Th: Then, look Don in the eyes, while he tells you again, and be sure whether he is being genuine.

Don: (sincerely) You are very important to me, and always have been.

Th: (to Nancy) How about now? (I am checking to see whether she now thinks he is being genuine).

Nancy: I still don't believe him, because there are times when he doesn't want to be with me.

Th: Why do you suppose that is? (I accept her reality as valid for her, and suggest that others can have their own motives, different from hers).

Nancy: Because I'm not important to him.

Th: Good, that's one possibility. Now think of another reason, another possible interpretation of why he might not want to be with you sometimes. (I imply that no one theory is ultimate, that there is always another option).

Nancy: (silence) ... I just think he doesn't care. Maybe he's distracted with other things.

Th: That's a possibility; he could be distracted with other things, like problems from work.... How about another possibility? (There is always another option to solve a problem, like the one Don has described as not wanting to be criticized).

Nancy: ... (silence) ... I don't know.

Th: Could I brainstorm with you about another possible reason? (My idea is not the ultimate answer, either, and you can make your own judgment about it).

Nancy: O.K.

Th: Perhaps he withdraws because he's afraid you might criticize him or make a derogatory comment about him. (The principle here is that condemnation of self or others is destructive, evoking a defensive response).

Nancy: That could be.

Th: (to Don) Is that a possible reason you back off sometimes? (Here I wanted Don to restate the complaint with which he began the session, checking for the possibility that he may not think the way I do).

Don: Yes, exactly. I really care about Nancy, but I don't like being criticized. She's important to me, and I don't see why she can't just wait until later to deal with things sometimes.

Th: You care about her, and don't see why she doesn't use the solution you use, to postpone dealing with something until you can give it your full attention. (Here I reframed his statement while mirroring it so as to identify his issue of wanting her to think the way he does and use his solution).

Don: Yeah.

Th: Will you tell Nancy again the truth about her being important to you? (I want Nancy to experience again the dissonance between her self-destructive assumption about not being important and Don's actual position of caring, which she discounts).

Don: (to Nancy) You are very important to me and I love you very much and I wish you would be willing to wait to deal with things until I can give you my full attention.

Nancy: I hear you saying that I should know you love me, and ...

Th: (Interrupting) The "should" is something you added that Don didn't say. Just pick up with "I hear you saying that you love me, and that I'm important to you ... " (I intervened to correct a destructive error Nancy was making by turning Don's expression of love into it's opposite, a critical injunction that Nancy "should" straighten herself out).

Nancy: I hear you saying (tears) . . . I don't think I can do this. . . . (softly crying) . . .

Th: (gently) I know it is difficult, but you can do it if you will. . . . (10 second pause) . . . You can cry and talk at the same time.

Nancy: (haltingly) I hear you saying you love me . . . (tears) . . . and you will always love me, and that I'm important to you even when you don't have time to talk to me . . . (tears).

Th: There is something sad about taking in what you've always wanted. . . . How would you describe your sadness? (I implied that her way of thinking is different from anyone else's way, and will mean more to her).

Nancy: I don't know. I just feel like crying. I don't know whether to believe him.

Th: Is it o.k. for Don to tell you again? (My goal is to communicate acceptance of her as she is, and repeat this process over and over, as long as she needs to be reassured that she is loved by Don).

Nancy: (Nods yes).

Don: (Therapist turns toward him). I love you and you're very important to me.

Nancy: (Still quietly crying, she nods, and seems to be more accepting of what Don said).

Th: Sometimes, when we get the love we have always wanted, we connect with the times in the past we have done without being loved, which is sad. (I am teaching her a way to think about her sadness, to use thinking as a way to solve problems and understand grieving).

Nancy: I don't know what I'm sad about from the past.

Th: Sometimes our sadness is not about what we had and then lost, but about what we should have had and never got. Grieving about what we should have had in the past opens the door to having what we want and need in the present. (More teaching about how to separate the past and the present, without discounting either).

Nancy: (Nods, still teary) I know what you mean.... It seems like we've just been talking about me, and Don hasn't been getting much from the session.

Th: I am glad Don has the opportunity to understand more deeply how important it is to you to know you count, that you are important to him. His understanding of you will help him be nurturing of you when you get scared. Like when, (looking at Don) in the first session we had, you spontaneously offered to drink less in the evenings because it bothered Nancy. (People learn from experience, and here Don has experienced in a new way the emotional importance to Nancy of her self-affirmation. He may have seen in a new way how important it is for him to reassure her of her value to him. In addition, he may see that his self-interest will be served as Nancy is less afraid and, as a result, she is less demanding of him).

Don: Yeah. (thoughtfully) I didn't understand the depth of this issue for you. I want to do whatever I can to help you as much as I can.

Th: (After a pause, to Nancy) What do you feel like doing, right now? (I sensed some affection nonverbally passing between Don and Nancy, and invited them to act on their emotions).

Nancy: . . . Taking a walk.

Th: Taking a walk. Where would you walk? (Give more details, because what you want is important).

Nancy: To the beach.

Th: Would anyone be with you? (Create the fantasy that would please you, since we always select what we do).

Nancy: . . . No, I'd be alone.

Th: (To Don) Would you like to go with Nancy? (He nods yes). Ask her and see what she says. (What she proposed -- being alone -- seemed to me to contradict the thrust of the session, that she does not want to be ignored and rejected and be alone. I guessed that her response about being alone was her old habituated response, and that she might be having difficulty asking for what she deeply wants, so as not to be hurt again).

Don: Would you like me to go with you?

Th: (Interrupting) May I make a suggestion? (Don nods yes.) Tell her, "I'd like to join you for a walk. Would you be willing for me to come along?" (This is part of their system of not asking for what they want by deferring to the other, as they did in the beginning of the session with deciding who will talk first. Since it is destructive from my point of view, I suggested a positive alternative).

Don: I would really like to go with you. Is that o.k. with you?

Nancy: (With obvious pleasure) Yes, I'd love it.

Th: (After a pause of about 10 seconds) Lets stop at this point tonight. You've done some hard work, and done well. (This seemed to me to be a natural closure, even though the session was not over).

Don and Nancy: (Simultaneously) Fine and o.k.

I identified within this session my assumption that Nancy's primary emotional issue was her discounting the value of what she had to offer. At times she also seems to regress to discounting the value of her existence. This illustrates the organic quality of our functioning, with dominant and minor themes both playing at the same time. While we can think of emotional development in a linear way, from childhood through adulthood, we actually live in an organic mix of what we have learned.

My other comments had mostly to do with the fifteen other assumptions related to quality and success in living. Throughout, movement toward emotional intimacy could also be understood as increasing their spiritual connection through sanctifying the emotional space between them. The words that are put into that space are powerful. They have a permanent, meaningful effect on the quality of the relationship.

How We Communicate Values Matters

What is communicated between therapist and client makes a considerable difference. In the following discussion, we show how value assumptions are expressed through the techniques various therapists use and the different ways that therapists actually treat clients.

The effectiveness of techniques is relative to the individuals with whom the therapist works. In *The Evolution of Psychotherapy* (p.12), Salvador Minuchin writes about how Carl Whitaker found as visiting professor at the Philadelphia Child Guidance Center that his techniques were frequently ineffective with the poor families he saw there.

In the same vein, he noted that Mara Palazzoli had the same problem, and that while her team was moving in the direction of developing a universal therapeutic strategy, their "therapeutic techniques must be grossly modified to be effective in the public sector with poor families" (p. 13).

The techniques of various schools of therapy, as well as the techniques of various therapists within a particular school, are immensely varied. This variation may be what leads us to speak of the "art" of psychotherapy, as a way to validate the effectiveness and legitimacy of various ways to do the work. The commonality that ties psychotherapy together does not rest in uniformity of theory or uniformity of technique. It almost seems as though when one creative mind comes upon a new and effective way of thinking about a particular therapeutic problem, that new way of thinking gives birth to a new therapeutic modality.

An example would be the development of the Alexander technique of bodily alignment that grew out of the work of F. Mathias Alexander in dealing with his own bodily misalignment (*Principles of the Alexander Technique*, 1999, by Jeremy Chance). His success, when generalized, has been of great help to others, and spawned a new therapeutic school and the training of a large number of therapists competent to teach others the results of Alexander's studies.

Instead of finding common ground in a common set of therapeutic techniques to be used with all clients, therapists may be able to find their universality as therapists based on underlying beliefs, assumptions that can be characterized as their underlying faith. We then use various tools technically to implement our understanding of what will be most useful to the client. If one approach doesn't work, we try another.

A commonality does exist among the operational assumptions that underlie the work of all therapists, even though the theoretical systems and technical maneuvers are so varied. Let us turn now to the three fundamental assumptions that underlie our psychotherapeutic work to show how they are present no matter what techniques are used.

First, the most basic assumption we communicate to clients is that they have intrinsic value, just because they exist, before they "do" anything.

1) COMMUNICATION TO THE CLIENT: YOU HAVE VALUE BECAUSE YOU EXIST.

Taking the client seriously in setting the initial appointment, and expressing a desire to be helpful, a therapist communicates the message, "You have value because you exist, even before we get acquainted."

We use a variety of techniques to communicate, all the while expressing our attitude toward the client in non-verbal as well as verbal ways. When the value of the individual is not the main focus of therapy, it is still supported in non-verbal ways.

The Hippocratic Oath rests on a belief in the value of the individual and a commitment (1) to do as a healer only what is in the interest of the healing of the patient, and (2) to eschew what is destructive in any form, to the best of the ability of the healer. This continues the tradition of valuing the individual.

Bruno Bettelheim's Commitment

In the world of psychotherapy, Bruno Bettelheim is a respected psychoanalyst who exemplified a commitment to the inherent value of each person. At one time in his clinical practice he opened his home to be a therapeutic environment for an autistic child, leading to his work in providing what he eventually called a *therapeutic milieu* in an institutional environment.

He describes his use of "therapeutic communication" to describe the environment he created for therapeutic work in *The Evolution of Psychotherapy* on page 228:

> "I toyed with the idea of calling it an extremely accepting situation, or an utterly benign environment. But since the purpose of our endeavor

> was therapeutic, I decided on the name *therapeutic milieu,* suggesting a setting in which everything is designed to promote the goals of therapy."

He set up an environment in which the individual was accepted and valued. A further quote will illustrate the depth of this commitment (p. 228):

> "A boy slowly returned to the world of the living and feeling when his caretaker--following some of the boy's acts--let him spread food on her bare arms, from which he then ate. Just as the infant feeds from the mother's breast, he had to return to feeding from the body of a mother substitute before he could begin to enjoy eating, and in slow steps, relating to and becoming a cherished part of this world."

A psychotherapist and teacher from a different tradition who built valuing the client explicitly into therapeutic technique is Carl Rogers. He describes "unconditional positive regard" as essential for therapeutic change. (The necessary and sufficient conditions of therapeutic personality change. *Journal of Consulting Psychology, 21,* 95-103).

Carl Rogers and Sandor Ferenzi

Rogers described the importance of relating to the client with empathy, entering into the personal world of the client to take seriously and understand what is of importance to that person. This seems to be a stance taken by any effective therapist, that of paying attention to and understanding the world of the client, by listening carefully to what is of importance to him or to her.

Earlier than Rogers, Sandor Ferenzi, who was a colleague of Freud, split from him to emphasize the importance of the positive, loving treatment of the patient in order to effect a cure based on increasing his or her self-esteem.

The therapeutic technique used by some therapists may be reflective listening as taught by Rogers, meant to communicate unconditional positive regard. Or, fantasy or gestalt exercises may be used to encourage the client to provide self-nurturing in the present, similar to what was missing as a child.

Focus on the Value of the Individual

Active listening, as taught in several therapeutic traditions, encourages the client to acknowledge the importance of the other person and to understand the meaning of his or her point of view. Mirroring in Imago Relationship Therapy expresses value of the individual by giving enough importance to the message being heard that it can be repeated almost verbatim.

In addition, homework to reinforce learning about self-worth may be given, such as writing on sticky notes, "I was born great," to be put on the bathroom mirror, in the wallet, on the steering wheel, and others in places chosen by the client.

Any number of other things may also be done by the therapist, congruent with his or her therapeutic model, that encourage the client to value himself or herself.

However it is communicated, this article of faith, the belief that people have value, is buried in whatever particular technique is used by the therapist, supported by the therapist's integration of the principle within his or her own personality.Even if the assumption that people have value is not explicitly spoken, the client will intuitively know if it is present or missing.

2) COMMUNICATION TO THE CLIENT: YOU MAKE DECISIONS FOR YOURSELF.

The second fundamental belief, that each person makes his or her own decisions, has many implications for therapeutic technique. One implication is that we do not make decisions for other people, and that we are not normally responsible for others' thinking, feeling, or behavior, except by agreement or in a crisis requiring immediate assistance.

As therapists, we can find ways to provide an environment that supports the client's experience of his or her autonomy. The experience that follows subjectively validates the inherent *value* of autonomous functioning. How autonomy is endorsed is the technique; the value is the article of faith that autonomy is desirable.

This principle of autonomy means that the client, not the therapist, is in charge of the decisions the client makes. The therapist will encourage the client to adopt the same position, using one or another therapeutic maneuver as the means to communicate the desirability of making one's own decisions.

Strategic Therapy

For example, in the context of a Strategic approach, the focus is on how to encourage the client to respond in a manner that will be positive for his or her well being. For example, an order from the therapist may be designed as a way to mobilize the rebellion of the client in order to make his or her autonomy eventually permanent without rebellion. The client might be told, for example, that "You must do what you are told (the implication being, unless you decide these things for yourself)." If the client already operates autonomously, orders from the therapist will be understood by the client as optional, a kind of assertive brainstorming to be used or dropped. Otherwise, rebellion may bring a positive result.

Psychoanalytic Therapy

A therapist trained to do psychoanalytic psychotherapy might use the technique of "agreeing with the resistance" to encourage and support a client's developing autonomy. The therapist agrees with the objections given by the client and then inquires how the person will deal with those objections in real life.

This leaves the client in charge, responsible to find the solution to his or her own problem, even though the unconscious inclination of the client may be to become more dependent upon the therapist, and attempt to get the therapist to come up with the "right" solution to the problem. The technique is one way for a therapist to endorse autonomy.

Transactional Analysis

In relation to autonomy, another illustration can be found in a clinical exchange described by Robert Drye, in *Techniques in Transactional Analysis*, Murial James, ed. He suggests a way of spotting the "rebellious child," a concept in Transactional Analysis theory, by being aware of the way the client may refuse to do what he or she is asked. The therapist can then invent an intervention that may help the client to reclaim his or her power to make decisions. The example given by Drye follows:

> "*Therapist:* "How are you feeling right now?"
>
> *Patient:* "Before I answer a question I like to think about it for awhile."
>
> *Therapist:* "Will you say: 'I don't want to answer your question' and see how that feels?"
>
> *Patient:* "I don't see how that would be useful."
>
> "I tell the patient that instead of saying 'no' or 'I won't' he gives me explanations for *not doing* what I'm asking. I bring his rebelliousness to his attention. His message seems to be 'I won't do what you want me to do when you want me to do it: maybe I will in my own good time when I'm ready.' " (p. 105)

The purpose here is to find ways to support the client's autonomy, and to aid the client to understand that he is in charge of what he does, even though he is so unsure that he attempts to make clear to himself that he does not have to do what the therapist wants. This learning is very much like what a two year old struggles to master by saying "no" when a parent wants "yes," or doing the opposite of what the parent wants. Adults, of course, perform the same behavior in a more sophisticated version. Either way, the purpose is the same: "If I do the opposite of what you want, I reassure myself that I am not being dominated by you."

The development of our autonomy is a universal human issue, and will inevitably show up to be dealt with in the therapist's office by the client for whom it is not resolved. Such a client will focus, in one way or another, on attempts to defend himself or herself from being dominated.

The therapist, in turn, will respond in some way to address this issue with the client. Whatever the therapeutic technique being utilized, the therapist will be taking a position, whether for or against the client making his or her own decisions.

The issue of autonomy is especially important in the therapeutic relationship because the structure of therapy encourages the client to be emotionally dependent on the therapist.

Therapy is An Emotionally Unequal Relationship.

There is a sense in which therapy is an emotionally unequal relationship from the point of view of the client, since the client is coming to the therapist expressly because he or she is not able to deal with some real life situations or because of personal emotional pain. Such pain may have come from abuse that reflects an unequal relationship as a child.

For example, when exploring the experience of physical or sexual abuse leading to current painful and disruptive symptoms, the therapist will listen to the client and respect what the client says, being careful to treat the client as an emotional equal.

This is especially important when abuse of some type is involved, since abuse can be understood as the unfair use of power by one person over another. It is important that the therapist not become another person using the power of an emotionally unequal relationship to abuse the client. For example, the therapist will avoid telling the client what to think and feel, as in "I know you were sexually abused, even though you don't remember it now."

With this emotional issue, as with all others, the therapist is a human being who has had to face and deal with the same fundamental issues as the client. The therapist may not have had experiences that were as traumatic as those presented by the client, but the therapist will have had to deal with the basic issues, since he or she is also a human being. No person escapes the developmental emotional issues and the need to deal with them positively. The emotional and spiritual learning of the therapist is what enables him or her to be a teacher and facilitator for the client.

No one can get inside the head of another and decide what is there. In order to support autonomy, we must listen and respect the pieces of the life-puzzle our clients share with us, invite them to make their own decisions, and encourage them to value their decisions, once made.

Whether autonomy is a primary issue of the client, as in passive dependent personality disorders, or an issue in the background as a client deals with how to be a separate person in a love relationship, it is a therapeutic issue to be respected, always with support in some form on the side of autonomy.

When a client is clear about his or her value and autonomy, comfortable in making decisions, the emotional issues to be addressed may then have more to do with the way in which those decisions are implemented. Let us explore how some techniques are used to affirm the right (and inevitability of) each person to act in his or her own way.

3) COMMUNICATION TO THE CLIENT: YOU THINK, FEEL, AND ACT IN YOUR OWN WAY.

The clinical application of this principle that we each have the right to think, feel, and act in our own way has varied forms. Whatever techniques are used by the therapist, when they are successful, they result in client behavior that supports the initiative of the individual or couple or family to be in charge of defining their own direction.

The message, "Your way to think, feel, and act is the only way you have" applies to many different everyday situations, but especially to taking initiative to *pursue* what one chooses. We are entitled to do things our own way, even though we are not perfect. Incorporation of some form of this belief by the client is addressed in a variety of ways by different therapists.

Family Therapists

Family therapists assume that "family secrets" are at least problematical, if not destructive, and that bringing them out into the open is beneficial. This therapeutic goal aims at endorsing the right of persons to have their own point of view or feelings or behavior, without the fear that requires hiding from others. After claiming the right to be different, individuals can negotiate solutions to conflicts related to those differences.

One example of a technique for accepting differences is Murray Bowen's suggestion to go and visit parents and grandparents in person in order to resolve old conflicts and disagreements as a foundation for an improved relationship. By granting the other person the right to be the way he or she is, by forgiveness, a schism may be healed. Such action initiates change in the family system in the direction of acceptance of differences as acceptable, since differences of some kind are inevitable.

Idealizing Transference

As another example of applying this principle of accepting people as they are, think of a person who may be overwhelmed by the stresses of life, may withdraw, stop functioning, and become depressed. One technique of supporting a person's self esteem, described by the psychoanalyst, Michael Basch, is to utilize the "idealizing transference" a client sometimes develops when asking for help from an expert.

In *Understanding Psychotherapy,* p. 36, Basch describes a patient with a

> "history of satisfactory functioning . . . overloaded with stress . . . had lost the ability to function effectively; his self-esteem had suffered in the process; and that, in turn, diminished his confidence in his decision making capacity and impaired his ability to halt his downward slide--the developmental spiral moving in reverse."
>
> He had the readiness for an immediate positive or idealizing transference: that is, he had available in his regressive state the hopeful attitude of a child who is able to look with trust to the powerful parent for assistance and relief. . . . Although I took an active role in the treatment I did not solve Dr. Osgood's problem for him but, rather, showed him what he had to do to regain his sense of competence."

By combining medication and management of his going back to work in small steps, the therapist helped Dr. Osgood regain his former level of functioning as a surgeon, reclaiming his self-esteem. The therapist directed the patient to take charge of his life again, using small steps that he could tolerate and re-integrate into his own life style, especially his work.

Lewis Wolberg

In *The Technique of Psychotherapy*, Lewis Wolberg suggests a way to invite the patient to function as an equal partner in the psychotherapy process, affirming the right of the patient to do things his own way. On p. 81, he says:

> "*Th.* There is no magic about getting well. The way we can best accomplish our goals is to work together as a partnership team. I want you to tell me all the important things that are going on with you and I will try to help you understand them. What we want to do is to develop new, healthier patterns. *My* job is to see what is blocking you from achieving this objective by pointing out some things that have and are still blocking you. *Your* job is to *act* to put into practice new patterns we decide are necessary, you telling me about your experiences and feelings."

This way, Wolberg communicates a respect for the initiative of the client in relationship to the therapist and the client's everyday living.

Erving Polster's Gestalt Therapy

Another technique, used in the context of Gestalt therapy by Erving Polster, is to encourage the client to exaggerate the feeling or behavior associated with the client's symptom. This exaggeration intensifies the emotional issue in order to explore how to deal with it more effectively.

Polster describes on p. 334 of *The Evolution of Psychotherapy* his work with a woman who would not express herself when she became angry with others with whom she disagreed. He writes:

> "That, she said, is what she was ashamed of--the dishonesty of her silence. . . .Her mother had always preached honesty at all costs, although when Ingrid practiced it her mother couldn't handle it. When lying was immoral and truth unpalatable, Ingrid, of course, found herself in a bind; she wound up silent over the years and forgot why."
>
> "In an attempt to flesh out the story, I suggested that, rather than stay stuck with the contradictions about truth, which only paralyzed her, she try an experiment in lying, assuring her it need be only for the moment. She got excited, transforming a worried look into one that was loose, even about the really tough week she had, working so hard around the house that her fingers split open and her nails crumbled. She 'cleaned at the office, watered plants, did lots and lots of work and lots and lots of reports, lots of letters'. . . . "

She then proceeded to tell a real story that paralled her imaginary story, about cleaning and cooking for company and not being appreciated by them, but herself appreciating how well she had done.

> "As it happened, in her family, men were allowed to go on and on about their experiences, some tall stories included, but the women were supposed to serve and tone themselves down. This realization clarified her shame about not being *counted.* By now though, she *felt* counted and her shame simply evaporated."

The self affirmation invited by and corroborated by the therapist led her to claim her right to be appreciated for her way and quality of doing things, fundamental to emotional health, as the antidote to her negative self-evaluation.

Other examples could be given to illustrate our faith in this operational assumption, that each person can only think, feel, and act in his or her own way, since that is the only way one has. The value of validation of one's own way, even when inadequate, is an article of faith we all seek to apply, whatever the theoretical framework or technical application.

Let us turn now to the four additional assumptions making up the second tier of values endorsed in psychotherapy.

4) COMMUNICATION TO THE CLIENT: YOU CAN ENJOY BEING THE PERSON YOU ARE, INCLUDING YOUR SEXUALITY.

Enjoying our own body is something we practice doing all our lives. Special and dramatic changes occur at adolescence, with the development of the ability to reproduce sexually.

Adolescence is a time for affirming and integrating adult sexuality and combining it with previous emotional learnings into a well-formed identity with which to live the rest of life. It is a time to put all the pieces of our life together in our own unique way.

Interpretation of Transference

Therapists communicate affirmation of sexuality as well as support for the individual to be his or her own kind of person, as fundamental values. Sometimes the technique of interpretation of transference is used to support a person, as in a case described by Wolberg on page 1108 of *The Technique of Psychotherapy.*

> "The interpretation of a transference reaction is especially helpful when correct. An adolescent boy treated his visits with me as a casual incident in his routine, refusing to talk about himself and waiting for me to do something dramatic to remove his facial tic. At one visit I remarked, 'You just won't say anything about yourself and your feelings. I get the impression that you don't trust me.' The patient's reaction was a startled one. He blushingly revealed that he was

embarrassed at his thoughts. He never was able to be frank with his family. Whenever he divulged any secrets to his brothers or his parents, they were immediately revealed to the whole family to his great embarrassment.

"When I retorted that there must be something about coming to see me that made him feel sheepish, he admitted wanting to ask me for some 'sex books' to explain masturbation and sex. Perhaps, I replied, he felt I might get the idea he wanted to stimulate himself pornographically with this literature. He blushed furiously at this, whereupon I reassured him that there was nothing to be ashamed of, that a strong sexual interest at his age was normal, and that I certainly would reveal nothing about our conversations to his parents. After all, what we talked about was between ourselves.

"This maneuver had the effect of releasing a flood of memories of incidents in which his confidence has been betrayed. Our sessions thereafter took a new direction with the patient participating actively."

The focus of the therapy moved on to other issues, supported by the belief that sexuality is normal and is to be affirmed. This is an article of faith that most therapists would probably endorse and support in their work with clients.

5) COMMUNICATION TO THE CLIENT: YOU CAN BE ON YOUR OWN AND A PEER WITH YOUR PARENTS.

The movement into adulthood involves the last vestiges of dependence on parents, usually monetary, but also psychological. The fundamental value held by most therapists is that it is desirable for a person to move into full psychological equality and economic independence in relation to his or her parents and spouse.

Transactional Analysis

One expression of this article of faith is found in a description by John Mackey of his work with a client using Transactional Analysis theory and methods. In *Techniques in Transactional Analysis*, p. 468, he writes:

> "Jerry entered treatment because he was having difficulty adjusting to the new liberated lifestyle of his wife, Linda. After seven years of relatively stable married life they were having many arguments and problems centered around her working and requiring that he give her more assistance with the house and children, and with her becoming more free to be sexual and to ask for sex for herself. . . ."
>
> "What emerged in our work was that Jerry had parents with the stereotypic relationship in which the father was a successful professional and mother was in charge of the home and children. We established that the basic message from mother was 'Don't disappoint me,' which

> covertly gave Jerry responsibility for mother feeling OK about herself as a mother. . . .When Jerry went to his father to discuss the college decision [he had made] his father's response was 'For Christ's sake, Jerry, can't you see that you've gotten your mother so upset that I can't think of anything now but getting her well.' "
>
> "Our work together moved from Jerry's taking care of himself, even if Linda was disappointed, and only subsequently into expanding his own options to include those which would please the 'new Linda.' The two of them worked on how to deal with the problem of Linda wanting freedom when Jerry didn't want to take care of the kids, and how they could relate to Linda's being sexually aroused when Jerry was not and didn't want to 'perform.' Compromise in the Adult was supported; adaptation was not."

The therapist supported Jerry's asserting his right to have equal recognition with his mother, father, and Linda, so that he need not comply with Linda's wishes to secure her love, but could learn to collaborate with her to take her wishes seriously without negating his own. He could be his own person, a peer with Linda, and be intimate on that basis.

6) COMMUNICATION TO THE CLIENT: YOU HAVE PERMISSION AND THE ABILITY TO CREATE.

Sometimes people come into therapy because of life crises that bring unresolved developmental issues to the fore. After establishing an ability to function as a capable adult, a person may become interested in venturing forth creatively. If children are not present, planning to have them may be an expression of creativity. Or the initiation of a business venture, or moving to a new career, or moving to a new location, or some other creative urge may become important.

The therapist will have some value orientation toward such changes, whether they are desirable or to be avoided. For example, it is an article of faith to believe that a person does well to follow the inner urges of creativity, matching them with the realities of current obligations and social functioning.

Clients in therapy exploring such issues may not have deeply rooted emotional conflicts, but need assistance in putting together what they already know about the importance of affirming their own interests, abilities, and personal goals in ways congruent with their own values.

An Eclectic Use of Techniques

One example is that of Albert, who came to psychotherapy complaining of mild symptoms of depression, such as sadness and irritability, changes in sleeping patterns, some inability to concentrate on his work, fatigue, and thoughts of suicide. At age twenty nine he was doing well in his work, completed an undergraduate college degree, had a fine family with three children, one in school, with whom he enjoyed spending time.

Albert's primary concern was his anger about personal failures. He was very self-critical when he did not perform according to his goals, even though his goals were reasonable, not perfectionistic.

In analyzing a dream in which he had not completed a task and had to go back to get additional tools, he concluded, "I don't want to be too assertive because I'll break the rules and lose my family." In his family of origin, the children had to follow his mother's expectations or she would be upset, emotionally hurt, and family life would be disrupted.

The therapist initially focused on encouraging Albert to cancel the self condemnation he engaged in related to others' displeasure in what he wanted or did when it did not hurt anyone. He then moved into acceptance of his own anger as legitimate.

The next step was creating a new way to relate to his wife and children in the mornings so they would have time to have breakfast together in an enjoyable way. He arranged this and was delighted with the positive change in the way his wife responded with warmth and pleasure.

The same ideas were useful in changing his way of relating to his co-workers, since he went home in the evenings to spend time with his family while they stayed on to work. He found he could negotiate a good working relationship with them, even though he did not follow their "rules." He applied the principles he already knew in a different fashion to improve his current functioning: one definition of creativity.

After fourteen sessions Albert began to talk about "graduation from his course in human relations and personal growth," so that by the seventeenth session he celebrated his integration of his new way of taking charge of his own life and the way he managed it.

He had affirmed the article of faith that he had the right and ability to reshape his life creatively as his life situation called for changes, and he terminated therapy joyfully. The evidence that he has solved earlier developmental issues present showed up as the ease with which he made the personality changes he found desirable to achieve. He was not afraid to change.

7) COMMUNICATION TO THE CLIENT: YOU CAN TEACH AND SHARE WHAT YOU HAVE LEARNED.

Some people choose teaching as a profession, and as a result teach much of their adult life. Others may find the urge to teach later in life. It may be that such teaching from what we have learned is a way to continue our spiritual connection with others, especially with the younger generation.

It seems a natural thing to share with others what one has found to be of value, and is intrinsic to the process of psychotherapy. By seeing a client, the psychotherapist is functioning in part as a teacher, and implicitly argues for the importance of sharing one's own knowledge to help the client grow. Teaching is one of many functions provided by a therapist.

Teaching as a Therapeutic Technique

Here is an example of how teaching a person to solve a current problem can also be understood as intrapsychic psychotherapeutic work with a powerful positive influence.

Evan, a 34 year old divorced man, set up an interview with a therapist to get some help solving a work problem. Evan had walked off his job when asked to do advanced mechanical work that was partly unfamiliar to him, requiring some skills and on the job training he did not yet have.

He had a history of walking out on jobs in the past after lengthy (two to five year) employment when asked to take a promotion to a position for which he was not fully trained.

In the first session he described his family history, including his alcoholic, physically abusive father, a mother who was compliant and ineffective, and a rebellious brother. By the age of 14 he had begun drinking and soon started experimenting with various drugs. He continued this pattern so that by the age of 30 he was on crack and was 50 pounds underweight. Searching for more crack was his only interest in life.

His mother, since divorced, sent him to a treatment center where he stayed for a year and he got off all drugs, and was "straight" at age 29, after divorcing his wife of 7 years, with whom they had a son.

The second session the therapist inquired about his parents, and he told how as a child he learned never to say, "I don't know" to his father, because when he did, his father would hit him on the head with his fist. He learned to be quiet and obedient so as not to be attacked by his father.

The therapist asked him if this fear of being hit felt similar in any way to his feelings when he left his job. He paused, thought a bit, and said, "Yes, just like I wouldn't be able to to the job because I didn't know how, and I would have to say, 'I don't know,' and then I knew I would be in big trouble."

He and his therapist discussed the ways in which his present boss is different from his father, and that *now he has not been and it is unlikely that he will be hit or punished for saying he doesn't know something.* In fact, his employer is eager to help him learn what he doesn't know, so as to increase productivity. He related this new understanding to three other occasions when he walked out on a job. He identified his pattern of running away and the principle that he can ask for information when he doesn't know the answer or doesn't understand. He began to believe that he never has to be "hit" again.

Evan thought about this for a week, and then spoke to his boss and arranged to go back to work at his original job, which he already knew well. By the time of the third therapy session, two weeks after the second one, he had been happily on the job for a week. He and the therapist discussed how he had succeeded in breaking the pattern of associating his boss and other authority figures with his father.

By the time of the fourth therapy session, two weeks later, he was doing well, including his working overtime, and doing the same relatively unfamiliar work he was asked to do previously when he fled from the job. This time, he explained, he asked for and got the information he needed to do the job correctly, when he didn't know how to do something. Here is an instance in which an educational approach was supportive enough of Evans intrapsychic change that he went ahead and changed his behavior. No doubt, Evan used the therapist as the good father he never had, giving emotional power to his new cognitive understanding.

Since he was doing so well, he and the therapist agreed to terminate therapy for the time being, leaving open the possibility for the client to call later to do further work on how to have a satisfactory relationship with a woman. Further therapy, if he chooses to do more, will be an opportunity to talk about what he doesn't know about relationships, an opportunity to learn without being criticized or attacked.

His parents were not equipped to teach him about how to have close relationships when he was a child. However, he has already succeeded in opening his life to new learning, even though he has not disturbed his underlying personality disorder related to avoiding intimacy.

Being able to teach others is a function of age, but it is also a function of wisdom, and hopefully wisdom grows with age. The older a therapist is, the more he or she may be seen as a model of the meaning of growing old for those younger. This powerful inter-generational statement may never be mentioned verbally, and yet is a "teaching" from therapist to client.

This article of faith says that teaching others what is positive is an important part of the psychotherapeutic process. The assumption that teaching others what is positive and useful has high value can be found in many different schools of therapy.

The point may even be self-evident since psychotherapy would not be considered by the therapist or client as worth doing if teaching and learning were not valued by both of them.

CHAPTER VI
CLINICAL APPLICATION OF THE FIFTEEN OTHER ASSUMPTIONS

These fifteen other assumptions are seldom explicitly mentioned by the client as part of his or her presenting complaint in an intake interview, while complaints related to the first three fundamentals are almost always present or implied in some form.

Yet these less fundamental principles are significant as operational assumptions since they directly affect the way in which life is lived and in which therapy is done. As a result, these beliefs affect the success of the client in achieving therapeutic goals.

In this chapter, the focus is on how the therapist applies these fifteen beliefs by using interventions and techniques that are congruent with them in the therapeutic process.

The fifteen beliefs are abstract concepts, that have therapeutic impact when they are translated into behavior (what the therapist says and does) by the therapist in relation to the client. It is primarily the therapist's *treatment* of the client (and the client's treatment of the therapist) that communicates these conceptually abstract values, not an explanation of the values to the client.

Some of the ways these concepts are translated into behavior is the focus of what follows. I treat each of the beliefs separately, with illustrations from the work of various therapists to show how they have an important impact on the process of therapy. My interpretation of their work may be different from what the clinician might say, further illustraing the difference between individual frames of reference. The examples simply serve to point to the fifteen operational assumptions, so that you, the reader, will be stimulated to develop your own point of view.

There are many ways in which each of these principles can be applied to facilitate the process of psychotherapy and make it more effective. In what follows, without attempting to be exhaustive, some applications to therapy used by various clinicians are presented in order to illustrate the clinical relevance of the assumptions. The reader may think of many other illustrations.

1) THE THERAPIST SUGGESTS WAYS THE CLIENT'S THINKING CAN INFLUENCE FEELINGS.

The belief that there is a difference between thinking and feeling shows up in therapy in various ways. One way is by the therapist inquiring about the thinking that precedes the client's unpleasant feelings.

The therapist may ask the client to identify thoughts, associations, or images that occurred just before he or she experienced panic, anger, or sadness. By identifying the linkage between thinking and feeling, the client achieves more control over thinking and indirectly more control over emotional responses, experiencing his or her power to modify thinking, feeling and behavior.

One example of the application of this idea is described by Arnold Lazarus, quoting a patient describing the onset of a panic attack:

> "'Things will be going along just fine, when I start *thinking* about all the different things that may go wrong. As I tune into each error, I can just *visualize* these things occurring. By that time, I notice that my heart is pounding away, my jaws are *tense*, and pretty soon I have a full-blown anxiety attack." (*Evolution of Psychotherapy, p.*171)

This knowledge of the difference between thinking and feeling may lead to reframing (thinking of) an issue in a way that is more positive emotionally. As part of the therapy, suppose a man learns that he can focus on all the things that can go well in his life instead of worrying about what might go wrong. He can think about how to deal successfully with whatever goes wrong. As he changes his thinking about his own ability to solve problems, his feelings will follow in a positive vein, giving him the subjective experience of control of both his thinking and his feelings.

The truth (which has to do with thinking, and judgment) is our "best friend," in a sense. To focus on the positives does not require a denial of or avoidance of the negatives. It simply defines a way of dealing with the negatives that might be considered problem solving. When we assume (thinking) that there is always another option to deal with difficulties, we focus on the positive potential without denying the existence of the problem to be resolved.

One way of stating this belief that there is always another way to solve a problem is that "Whatever happens I can deal with it." The ultimate aphorism of this point of view would be "I'll die with my boots on," going for a positive solution. Whatever happens, even death, will not shake that person from focusing on how to achieve the positive.

When a problem cannot be solved in any other way, as with the impossibility of reversing the death of a loved one, the only remaining "solution" is to grieve about the loss and move on to other things. Even here the focus is on the positive process of dealing with loss in a way that is in harmony with human nature.

Making a new decision to modify old ways of solving problems in Transactional Analysis Redecision theory uses thinking to re-evaluate reality, resulting in the modification of difficult feelings. Psychoanalytic practice uses thinking to re-interpret the meaning of emotionally intense experiences in the light of present knowledge. The new understanding results in a modification of feelings and a new connection between thinking and feeling (state dependent learning). Other successful technical approaches share the same faith-belief that a modification of thinking can change feelings.

2) THE THERAPIST SUGGESTS CHANGES IN BEHAVIOR IN ORDER TO MODIFY FEELINGS.

The therapist who believes there is a difference between thinking and feeling will also make a distinction between thinking/feeling and behavior. It is usually assumed that changes in thinking and feeling will result in some modification of behavior, as when a person is not afraid, he or she does not behave in defensive ways. A change in behavior may result from changes in the endocrine system or may occur in response to experiences that modify one's interpretation of the situation. As a result, feelings change in response to the changed interpretation and behavior.

It is useful to know that changes in behavior will affect feelings. Positive changes in behavior may, by themselves, evoke positive feelings by association with previous experiences, resulting in a willingness to take further positive action (using mechanisms of state dependent learning).

Based on these ideas, a therapist may make suggestions to a client about ways to act differently that will affect his or her intrapsychic emotional system. By behaving differently, a person may experience different thoughts and feelings. At times, the change may provoke more anxiety, when the change is experienced as a "breaking of the old rules of behavior" that previously guaranteed some safety. At other times the client may simply make changes in behavior that "work better" than what he or she had done before, and integrate the new behavior into everyday living without anxiety. An example of this latter process follows.

William Glasser, in *Reality Therapy*, describes a client who changed her behavior as her way to achieve emotional change:

"Recently Margaret, a patient who had been coming once a week for a year, asked to come every other week because she felt so much better able to cope with the world than she had in the past. When I agreed that she was ready to come less often she tried to put into words what had happened that led to her doing so much better. . . . 'We seemed to have talked very little of what was important, but now I feel much better, and many things which I couldn't do, I am now able to do well.' She asked me if I knew what had happened. I told her that we talked about what was really important, that I had always pointed out reality, and that I had never accepted her irrationality, promiscuity, or depression as excusable ways of coping with her world. Rather than looking for *why* she was the way she was, I had made sure that she knew *what* she was doing. Margaret was motivated to change *because* nothing dramatic had been dredged from her subconscious, *because* her irresponsible past had been left alone, and because her fits of depression and promiscuous acting-out had not been excessively discussed. . . . Emphasized were her daily behavior, what she did rather than what she felt, and whether she could do better" (pp. 41-42).

This article of faith affirming the difference between feeling and behavior is found in the technique of many psychotherapists, expressed in different ways. The effect of behavior on thinking and feeling is so "obvious" that most of us do not stop to think about it, but just act as if it is true. For example, runners will affirm that their running behavior is very positive. It is true because it works in a positive way.

3) THE THERAPIST ENGAGES THE CLIENT EMOTIONALLY, TO GIVE POWER TO CLIENT CHANGES.

The therapist who believes that emotions provide energy to act, positively or negatively, will seek to engage the client emotionally in ways that support positive change. This implies more than theoretical discussion. It implies that the therapist will make emotional contact with the client. Following is an example from gestalt therapy of one way this principle can be applied.

Erving Polster describes a woman who had grown up as a waif in New York, who was promoted to an executive position and found herself with a manipulative secretary who presented herself as a victim to be placated. The executive, whom we will call Janis, had been aware of viewing her younger brother and others for whom she had caretaking responsibility as waifs, not seeing herself as a waif.

She had a newly employed secretary who wanted to be taken care of, evoking in Janis a sense that in some way she had always secretly seen herself as someone to be taken care of, as a waif. Janis wanted to replace that image of herself with an image of herself as a grown up woman.

Polster describes part of a therapy session on p. 74 of *Gestalt Therapy Now,* after the client had just become aware of her view of herself as needing caretaking:

> "As she told me about this, a new look came over her face, a mixture of absorption, alert introspection, and yielding to puzzlement. When I asked her what she felt, she said in surprise that she felt a tightness in her breathing and in her

legs. She concentrated on these sensations and after a few moments of silence looked surprised again and said she felt a tightness in her vagina. I asked her to attend to this sensation, which she did. Again, after a few moments of concentration a brightness arose in her face, and she said the tightness was leaving. Then she seemed startled and suddenly had a deep sensation that she didn't describe but instead burst into paroxysms of crying, calling out the name of a man she loves and with whom she has for the first time had a relationship of mutuality and strength. When she looked up, there was great beauty and wholeness apparent in her. As we spoke further, she realized the importance of her confrontation with her secretary, whom she subsequently fired, and the rediscovery of her feelings about waifs. But she knew that her deepest breakthrough came with the discovery of the sensation in her vagina. The subsequent awakening of her palpable feelings of womanhood gave substance and therefore primal resolution to problems which might otherwise only be verbalized."

The willingness of the therapist to support the client's awareness of her feelings and bodily sensations gave emotional power to her newly modified self-concept that she was no longer a waif, but a competent woman. Awareness of her feelings converted her abstract concept of herself as a waif into a deep experience of herself as a woman instead of a child. She used her cognitive ability to appreciate the significance of the experience. Polster's belief in the power of the emotional process helped her achieve this breakthrough.

4) THE THERAPIST ALLIES WITH THE CLIENT'S ABILITY TO THINK AS A WAY TO FACILITATE CHANGE.

The belief that thinking provides a tool for solving problems is one belief underlying the process of psychotherapy. The difficult task for the client and therapist is to use thinking to re-interpret the meaning of painful and problematical emotional experiences and then design improved ways to deal with them. Based on the assumption that emotional energy helps a client change, linking thinking *and* feeling is more effective than focusing on either thinking or feeling separately.

Storytelling is one powerful way to link the affective to the cognitive as a means to utilize thinking ability to make emotional changes, especially with small children, who still use concrete operational thinking. Children understand storytelling, because they have usually been told or read stories. Stories engage the child's imagination and feelings.

Richard Gardner, a master in using storytelling techniques, tells of a therapy session he had with Chris, age 5 1/2, who was having difficulty with other children teasing him because of his harelip. Chris thought of himself as very ugly, and wrote a note to Dr. Gardner, saying "I think god hates me because of my lip, and when I die he'll probably send me to hell." As the therapy progressed, Gardner told a story to Chris, as follows (pages 679-680 of *Therapeutic Communication with Children)*:

> "Once upon a time there was a person who went out and saw something. It was a plant and it had a little mark on it. Then the plant said to the man, 'I know that everyone hates me for this

mark that I have on me, for this small mark which I have. So go away and don't bother me.' Then the man said, 'Yes, I see the mark, but I can hardly notice it. To me you're a very beautiful plant, and I'd like to take you into my house.'

"The plant didn't believe it. He was very mad because he thought that he was ugly all over and he kept telling people to go away.

"Then the plant met a bigger plant who had a similar line and mark on his petal. And the two began to speak. The little plant said, 'Don't you think you're ugly all over?' What do you think the big plant then said?

"*Patient:* No.

"*Therapist:* Why?

"*Patient:* 'Cause he didn't care about it.

"*Therapist:* Why else?

"*Patient:* It doesn't make the whole self ugly.

"*Therapist:* Right! So what did the little plant think then?

"*Patient:* He was happy.

"*Therapist:* Was he mad anymore?

"*Patient:* No.

"*Therapist:* Do you know what the lesson of that story is?

"*Patient:* One little mark doesn't make you ugly all over.

"*Therapist:* That's right, perfectly right. A little mark in one place is hardly noticeable, but even if people notice it they just think that you have a little mark in one place. They don't think it makes you ugly all over. But if you think that one little mark makes you ugly all over you will feel bad about yourself, it may make you quite mad. . . .

> "Chris needed only a few more sessions for the treatment of his exaggerated reaction to teasing. . . . He was also handling those who occasionally teased him. He would either tease them back or respond with a comment like: 'You must be some kind of a nut to laugh at somebody just because he has a little mark on his lip. . . ' In our last session, Chris told me that he had changed his mind and that he no longer felt that God hated him."

Belief in the importance of the therapist-client alliance is powerful. That alliance, when applied to thinking, need not call on highly abstract concepts, but may be very concrete, as with Chris. Concrete ideas connect with emotions in a very natural way.

The essential part is the cognitive re-framing that gives a new meaning to affective experience. That new meaning is linked to the resulting new feelings and tends to result in new forms of behavior.

Chris modified his theology (his thinking about God) through his therapy experience. One could dismiss the change as the anthropomorphism of an immature child. And one could also interpret the change in his concrete theology from "God hates me" to "God doesn't hate me" as a spiritual experience mediated through his contact with Dr. Gardner. Both ways of viewing Chris' changed view of God would capture the same truth.

Being in harmony with the truth is the essence of positive spirituality.

The impact of the therapist upon the client can be powerful. It is always significant.

5) THE THERAPIST NOTICES PHYSIOLOGICAL, EMOTIONAL, AND INTERPERSONAL FACTORS IN THE CLIENT.

An assumption made by many therapists is that people are not a collection of parts, but make up an organic whole. The expertise of the therapist is important in dealing with the person as an organic whole.

The way in which physiological, emotional, and interpersonal factors influence each other may be very complicated and difficult to sort out for a client. The therapist can be a helpful guide, as well as the person to aid the client in using his or her inner wisdom and resources to resolve issues and redefine how to act in everyday life experiences.

John J. O'Connor, in his chapter on "Strategic Psychotherapy" in *Psychotherapist's Casebook*, (Kutash and Wolf, eds.), describes in some detail his work with Michael, a ten year old who had been referred by his pediatrician because of his preoccupation with and fear of vomiting. His pediatrician had conducted extensive testing to rule out organic medical problems.

He was an anxious child, overprotected by his mother, with few friends, and was very sensitive about the condition of his body. At one time after having a blind substitute teacher, he became concerned whether he would lose his teeth, hair, and eyesight.

O'Connor met with the family five times over three months, and describes his interventions:

> "I told him [Michael] that I knew how desperately he wanted to master the fears and thoughts and that although the tasks would be difficult, . . .I thought these tasks would help. . . .

"I then told Michael that the first step in mastering his fear of vomiting was to take charge of when and where he would vomit or think about vomiting. I told him . . . I wanted him to sit in a kitchen chair for one hour daily, to think hard about trying to vomit, and to mop it up if he did. At other times, if he began to think he would vomit, he should 'give' those thoughts to the hour and chair in which he would sit. He should say to himself, 'I'll think and worry about it then.'

"I then asked Michael's father to give me a button he had pinned on his sweater. I told Michael that this was his father's button and would represent his father's strength and reassurances. . . . His father was not to verbally reassure him in the morning but could ask whether Michael had his button.

"As part of Michael's learning, . . . I stated that the parents should obtain a sitter and go out one evening during the week for at least three hours. . . . I also indicated that, as part of Michael's developing age appropriate skills and mastery over his body, he should be required to perform certain tasks around the house, as other ten-year-olds do, and that his parents were to agree on what responsibilities they would require of him" (pp. 499-500).

These directives were based on an analysis of Michael's individual system, the family system, and the therapeutic system. Without attempting to restate the rationale for the directives, discussed in some detail by O'Connor in the chapter, we can see that the experience of the therapist was brought to bear on the situation in a way that was helpful.

Michael's symptoms began to diminish as the family and he carried out the directives of the treatment, and by the third month, he was "asymptomatic, not complaining to his parents, visiting, and having friends over; there was no mention of his fear of vomiting.

Behaviorally, he appeared more at ease and less tense. . . . In a two-year, follow-up phone call, mother indicated that Michael was 'doing terrifically.' He was achieving good grades in school, had a larger network of friends with whom he visited and spent overnights, and was not complaining about any obsessions or fears to his parents."

It is the therapist's experience that provides ideas and stimulation to explore issues in ways that are helpful and to make changes in ways that work, without the client having to learn experimentally from the beginning, to "re-invent the wheel."

By being aware of the physiological, emotional, and interpersonal factors in the client, the therapist can provide a wholistic perspective that the client may have difficulty being aware of while dealing with the particularly painful experiences that led to therapy.

The therapist's belief in the systematic nature of our emotional functioning is part of the expertise, whatever his or her theoretical orientation, that is brought to bear in ways that are helpful to the client, and can be appreciated by therapists from other theoretical orientations.

6) THE THERAPIST OPPOSES CONDEMNATION OF SELF AND OTHERS AS DESTRUCTIVE.

Assuming that self-condemnation or condemnation of others is destructive puts the therapist on the side of affirmation of the positive rather than criticizing the negative.

Criticism may come from others but when it is most destructive it comes from oneself, when a person gives the condemnation power by agreeing with it. Whether the criticism and condemnation is from others or from oneself, it is a "change of subject" from the undesirable event to focus instead on the failure and inadequacy of the person who created the event.

Self-condemnation may take the form of shame about oneself being unacceptable or the form of guilt in response to negative events ideas, or feelings.

When shame is the issue, the self-condemnation focuses on the *existence* of the person, as if to say, "You shouldn't be the way you are." This form of self-negation is never constructive and is always destructive.

When guilt is the issue, the self-condemnation focuses on the *behavior* of the person, as if to say, "You shouldn't have done what you did."

There is one way in which self criticism can serve a constructive purpose. That is when a person violates his or her own values, so that the guilt or self criticism raises a danger flag that says, "Think again; this is not your way of doing things." The destructiveness comes when the person must be "bent out of shape" to conform by negating values such as those described in this book.

Sometimes, over a long course of therapy, both issues may be dealt with. John, a 45 year old veteran, retired from a career in the Navy, and went back to school to become a social worker. He grew up in a blue collar section of a large city, and had hard working parents with little time to give to him, his brother, and sister. His mother was verbally very critical and his father physically abusive.

John came to therapy complaining of depression, because "no matter how hard I have tried to please my mother, my bosses, my wife, and others, I end up thinking I'm no good." This issue was the theme for a year of therapy, with John gradually coming to understand and believe that his value as a human being was not contingent upon his mother's or others' approval of him.

As he changed, he simultaneously became less compliant to others' wishes and less inclined to attempt to control others. He began to understand that he had chosen his second career partly to satisfy his personal need to be valued by others.

As therapy progressed, he became more independent, and began to focus more on others' evaluation of the way he did things. "I'm afraid when my wife gets angry that she will reject me, so I think of ways to please her. But whatever I do, it never seems to be enough to keep her happy."

With his social work agency superiors, he was careful to avoid conflict, by doing what he was supposed to do. This was more difficult than it had been in the Navy, where the structure was more well defined and he knew what was expected. Being very intelligent, he rose easily through the ranks.

John needed another year of therapy to begin to integrate into his everyday life the idea that he could value his own way of doing things, that he is highly intelligent, not dull, and that disagreements and conflicts with others can be negotiated without the violence he experienced with his father, or the cold withdrawal he received from his mother.

In fact, he began to perceive that differences between people can be an opportunity to enjoy and learn from them, and are not necessarily an occasion for more rejection and criticism.

The reason he was so cautious in this process was his own inner self-condemnation, first that he was no good for anything, and also that whatever he did, thought, or felt was so basically flawed that no one would want him around for long.

He was delighted to find that both of these self-condemning beliefs were his misunderstanding growing out of his relationship with his parents, and were not an accurate description of himself or the way people he cared about treated him.

He spent considerable effort replacing his self-condemnation with valuing himself and appreciation of what he has to offer others. It is quite difficult to modify a lifelong pattern of self-denigration.

When a mistake is made or an error occurs, the negative consequences provide enough motivation to examine what went wrong and find a way to correct it. Self-condemnation gets in the way, since it focuses on punishing the wrongdoer rather than correcting the error or righting the wrong that was done. As as result, self-condemnation is often an element in depression, contributing to a vicious circle of more depression.

7) THE THERAPIST FOCUSES ON EXPERIENCE AS A RESOURCE TO CORRECT WHAT WENT WRONG AND TO BUILD ON WHAT WENT RIGHT.

The assumption that people learn from their own experience suggests that the therapist view the client's experience as a set of learning tools to correct what went wrong in the past and to build on what went right. Upon examination, new understanding of past events can be developed, and new methods of dealing with similar situations in the present and future can be developed.

One way of describing this principle is described by Ernest Rossi as psycho-biological psychotherapy, "a means of accessing and therapeutically reframing the state-dependent mind-body processes that encode problems (*What is Psychotherapy*, Jeffrey K. Zeig, ed., p. 356)." He goes on to show how he applies the concept, using hypnotic techniques.

He illustrates the process of therapeutic intervention with the case of an overworked physician in his mid-forties with chronic migraine headaches, backaches, and a stiff neck, as follows.

> "The first step is *accessing the source of the problem*. . . . When, with a forlorn look, he finally paused for a breath, I . . . said, 'Hold your hands up like this, about eight inches apart. If your unconscious has some understanding of the source and solution of these problems, you'll find those hands coming together all by themselves. Otherwise, you'll find them being pushed apart.'
>
> "Incredulous at first, he became delighted as his hands moved slowly together. . . . I continued with: 'And if your unconscious is ready to

provide you with the *necessary emotional understanding of the sources of those problems so you can resolve them here and now,* you'll find your eyes closing all by themselves.' After a few blinks, his eyes closed and his face relaxed as he spontaneously took a deeper breath.

"The second step is *therapeutically reframing a state-dependent problem.* I continued with: 'And if your unconscious can now review the entire history of those problems, privately within your own mind, one of those hands will begin to slowly lower all by itself with each significant memory that is reviewed.' Slowly, one hand lowered to his lap as a gamut of emotions moved across his face: flushing, tears, and so forth. . . .

"The third step is *facilitating continued self-healing.* When his hand reached his lap, I asked if he was feeling comfortable, and he nodded his head agreeably. . . . I concluded: 'When your unconscious and conscious minds know they can continue with this inner healing, you'll find yourself awakening, feeling refreshed and alert.'

"He 'awakened' and confirmed that he was indeed symptom-free" (pp. 357-359).

In this therapy session, Rossi first asked if the client could tolerate knowing the source and solution of his problems. Getting a "yes," he then asked if he was willing to change. Getting another "yes," he invited him to review how the problem was to be resolved. Then he suggested continued healing.

We can see the therapist's confidence in and reliance on the client's resources to solve problems and the function of the therapist in assisting the client in accessing and using those resources.

8) THE THERAPIST DEFINES MOVEMENT TOWARD COOPERATION AND CLOSENESS AS DESIRABLE AND HEALTHY.

Believing that human beings are social animals leads a therapist to support cooperation and closeness as desirable and healthy. This idea is also the basis for the life-giving significance of people being in contact with each other, the profound experience of spirituality and engagement with all humanity.

Bill came to therapy with his wife, Jill, because of her complaints about his being distant, shutting her out by not coming home when expected and not answering her phone calls. She also wanted more physical affection. He was somewhat guarded, but seemed to have some interest in resolving her discomfort.

Bill is a twenty seven year old engineer who grew up in a family with a hard-working father and a mother who was a traditional housewife, staying at home to take care of him and his two younger brothers. His parents cared about each other, but did not express affection physically and did not communicate about personal matters, at least in front of the children.

His father made most of the decisions in the household. His mother would cope well with an emergency, as when taking him to the hospital with a broken arm, but would then "fall apart" after handing him to the doctors.

In therapy sessions, mostly joint with Bill and Jill, the therapist and Bill discussed the importance of communication and emotional closeness. He said, "I want to be closer to Jill, but I don't know how to do it. Sometimes I want to talk to Jill and have her only listen, and not interrupt." She agreed to do so, and they were given homework to spend time each evening with one telling something and the other carefully listening, so as to understand. This seemed helpful even though they succeeded only three nights out of seven.

The next session, Bill brought up a new subject. Speaking to Jill with some frustration, he said, "When you're upset I have to fix it." Jill responded with, "But I just want you to listen and understand when I'm upset. You don't have to fix it." Being listened to, of course, is the same thing that Bill had said that he wanted from Jill, giving them a basis for being allies in the quest for mutual acceptance and understanding.

The therapy continued, with the therapist supporting Bill's ability to be close without giving away his autonomy, relating this issue to his mother's intrusiveness and her requirement that he be close and compliant. As Bill put it, "I'm entitled to say how much I express and how much I don't."

At one point, when encouraged by Jill to be more forthcoming with his ideas and feelings, he said, "Don't push me. I'm trying to reverse thirty years of being guarded." Jill, of course, had her own complementary issues related to her need to start with a distant partner who she could convince to become more warm and loving, as a way to resolve her own "leftover" issues with her distant father.

Even though he wanted more closeness, Bill was frightened that the cost would be his own independence. He was inclined to slip back into his old defense of his autonomy by creating emotional distance as he did with his mother, who wanted to "manage" his life. The therapist is in a unique position to support closeness as an independent choice and to model respect for the client's autonomy in the process.

Whatever the clinical issue, the therapist operates from the position of faith that intimacy in a relationship is preferable to cutoff and isolation. As a result, the therapist will take the position that it is desirable for a couple to be cooperative with each other, and that emotional intimacy is more desirable in a marital relationship than emotional distance. We may not usually think of these ideas as values, but they are fundamental assumptions used by most therapists.

9) THE THERAPIST SUPPORTS THE CLIENT TAKING RESPONSIBILITY FOR DECISIONMAKING.

One of the most common issues in emotional growth is that of taking responsibility for one's own thoughts, feelings, and actions. This is where our power to act lies, in our own decision making, not in making decisions for others (unless we have a contract to do so, as in the military).

One of the interesting facts about this principle is that we already do make our own decisions by selecting what we say or do, even when we choose to follow others' directions.

The assumption that we always select what we say or do puts the responsibility for the doing on the shoulders of the doer. Making decisions in this sense may not be self-conscious, something we are aware of doing, yet the decision takes place within the brain and body of the person deciding.

The selection of what to do may be made in the primitive or "reptilian" brain, out of conscious awareness, but it is still the brain of the person deciding what to do next.

Richard Gardner described his work with Charles, an eight year old with severe immaturity problems, about six months after his mother's death from leukemia (pp. 527-529 of *Therapeutic Communication with Children)*:

"*Patient:* Can you help me [begin the story]?

Therapist: Well, all right I'll help you start the story and then when I point my finger at you you say exactly what comes to your mind.

Once upon a time a long, long, long time ago

in a distant land far, far, far away there lived a -----

Patient: Car.

Therapist: And this car ——

Patient: Helped all the people cross the street. It was like a mechanic. Then one day the car went into a crash. Its name was Auto. So all the lights were broken and the children didn't know how to cross the street. So they all got sad. So a man fixed the Auto's car and they were back to normal.

And the lesson of that story is: you should always know how to cross the street because when you go to school you're going to have to cross the street and if nobody's helping you, oh, you're in a lot of trouble."

Gardner continues:

"The car named Auto represents the patient's mother who had died a few months previously. She had been his 'guiding light,' and, as the story demonstrates, when she dies in an automobile accident in which the car's lights are broken, the children are left without guidance—'they don't know how to cross the street. . . . '

With this understanding of the patient's story, I told mine:

"*Therapist:* Once upon a time there were these kids and these kids used to depend a lot on a certain car. That car did lots of things for them. It used to take them to different places, even to short distances where they could really walk or ride their bike, and it would often light their way across the street, even when it wasn't that dark....the kids gradually realized that this car wasn't doing them very much of a favor because they weren't learning to do things on their own. . . .So gradually they decided only to use the car in emergency situations and they felt much better about themselves after that, because they had learned to do these things on their own.

"And the lesson of that story is when you learn to do something on your own you feel very good about yourself. . . .

"Did you understand what that story was about? What did your understand the lesson of that story to be?

"Patient: Well, it was like when somebody who always crossed you and they die then you have to learn to do it all by yourself. You feel good if you learn to do things by yourself."

Dr. Gardner is explicit about his endorsement of competence and self-esteem, expressing an underlying article of faith that we select what we do, and that selecting competence is better than choosing helplessness. He concludes, "In my story I referred to the mother's overprotectiveness . . . I stressed the important relationship between competence and self-esteem. My moral reiterates the same message."

His acknowledgment of a "moral" in his story is the acknowledgment that he is inviting Charles to agree with his values and reclaim his self-confidence. He is "selling" his positive message to Charles, with the confidence that it will be healing for him.

10) THE THERAPIST SEES BEHAVIOR AS A WAY TO COMMUNICATE WITH OTHERS.

Another assumption is the belief that we are always doing something. When we describe our behavior as doing "nothing," we are either hiding the truth or describing our passivity. Sometimes passivity is used as a way to say "no" without saying it out loud, so it is useful for the therapist to understand that the behavior of the client communicates something important as a basis for cooperating with the client's goals.

The following illustration describes the way Milton Erickson applied the principle that we are always doing something, and that what we do has a meaning. It is one of Erickson's talents that has enticed so many therapists to study his work and learn more about his ability to "read" others' communications. On p. 132 of *Healing in Hypnosis* he writes:

> "I am thinking of a patient I saw for Dr. Pearson. The gentleman said to me, 'I want you to hypnotize me,' meanwhile giving me a very, very cold shoulder in body language. I acted as if I believed he actually wanted me to hypnotize him. That patient was not aware of his own unconscious resistances.
>
> "When I asked, 'Do you want me to hypnotize you in a light trance, a medium trance, or a deep trance?', he crossed his legs and brought his hands way over to the side--drawing himself even further away from me--and answered simply that he thought a deep trance would be the better trance! Well, I could see the real meaning of that behavior. I acted as if I believed every word that man had said, but I also knew that he would not

be about to go into a trance. My task was to get him to recognize that what he really needed was not a trance by me, but psychiatric help. When I initiated this topic he immediately turned around to face me squarely and proceeded to talk about his need for psychiatric help."

Our behavior communicates as much or more than our words, and forms an important part of our communication with others. Our behavior includes our gross physical movements, and it also includes our speech, the inflection in sounds we make, and gestures so subtle they are hard to identify.

In addition, as we are taught by the object relations theorists, even our emotional position may evoke a response from another without our having to "do" anything, as in projective identification. Of course, this communication could be interpreted as transmitted through behavioral means, such as a tilt of the head, a cast of the eyes, and so on.

However described, another article of faith for therapists is the belief that our own and the client's behavior are part of the therapeutic dialogue.

11) THE THERAPIST KNOWS THE WAY THE CLIENT IS TREATED HAS POWERFUL EFFECTS.

One application of the principle that what we do affects others is the idea that what a therapist does and does not do with a client has an important effect on the client. Mary M. Goulding, being aware of this, put the idea provocatively in her book (*The Power is in the Patient)* in the chapter "To My Clients:"

> "I am bored with pathology. I am excited by health. And growth.
>
> "Tell me your troubles, confusions, mistakes, hates, and I'll listen for as short a time as possible; therefore, I'll treat you as fast as I can. Tell me of your triumphs and I'll hear you out. And applaud every word....
>
> "I am not interested in your sucking in my protection, permission, or potency. My potency is: I give me to be with you in health, in growth, so that you, too, will discard in boredom your pathology and celebrate yourself in health" (p. 15).

No doubt, her point of view has an impact on her clients, and that has an effect on the way they respond to her in treatment. She is clearly committed to health and growth. She is quoted here to illustrate that each of us has *some* way we view clients and therapy, whatever it may be, and the way we live out our view affects the clients with whom we work.

In a similar way, how the client treats the therapist affects the therapist, and influences the response the therapist will make.

The client may influence the therapist to respond in a way the client unconsciously desires. This process is described as “projective identification” in object relations theory. For example, the client may unconsciously relate to the therapist in such a way as to encourage the therapist to respond to him or her as a victim in need of rescuing, as a way to maintain a psychological position learned as a child.

Many of our habituated responses are "built into" our personalities, so that we automatically respond in characteristic ways to the same sort of stimuli. We have a kind of “blueprint” of the way things are, including our thoughts, feelings, and behavior in response to the way things are. The therapist faithfully believes that we have the ability to become aware of our automatic responses, evaluate them, and choose to change them, if we wish to do so.

12) THE THERAPIST ENDORSES THE FUNDAMENTAL VALUES THAT ENCOURAGE GROWTH AND HEALTH.

Acknowledgment of the assumption that we all have values and use them as criteria for action leaves us with the question of how we apply them as therapists. Hopefully, we have values that support growth and health, whatever our definitions of growth and health may be.

At one time, many therapists proposed taking a value-neutral stance with patients, on the assumption that it is possible to take such a position with the patient never knowing the values of the therapist. This approach, part of psychoanalytic theory, may have succeeded in achieving anonymity of the values of the therapist to some degree, while at the same time communicating the value of passivity and emotional distance. But some values "leak out," whether verbally expressed or not.

Milton Erickson is a therapist who expressed his own point of view to clients, in such a way as to respect the values of the client. He took people where they were and used his understanding to "cooperate" with them to achieve some positive purpose.

For example, he describes the way he helped a client mitigate his extreme guilt over having extramarital affairs. The value being endorsed is that guilt is destructive and that the man would be better off solving his problems by some means other than his affairs:

> "I think the way to handle that man's guilt is to teach him to have less guilt reactions about his extramarital affairs. He ought not to have guilt about extramarital affairs. Do you see the

> transformation there? *He ought to have less guilt about his extramarital affairs. . . . he really ought to have less guilt. . . . he ought to have no guilt at all.* I am seemingly encouraging him to have those extramarital affairs with less guilt, but as he works on my suggestion in accord with the needs of his own personality, *he's going to start lessening the number of his extramarital affairs in order to lessen his guilt.*
>
> "You ought to know what goal you have in mind for the patient. In having that guilt reaction, the man was asking me to do something about the correction of his extramarital affairs. But if I had tried to tell him, 'Now, cut out those affairs . . . don't be a bad boy . . . that's bad behavior,' then I would have failed in the therapeutic purpose" (*Life Reframing in Hypnosis*, p. 208).

Erickson was able to understand the point of view of the patient, and then intervene in ways that would stimulate the patient to respond positively, as Erickson defined it. In his own way, he encouraged acceptance of values that he viewed as supportive of emotional health, something all therapists do in their own way as well. He acted on that in which he believed to be in the best interest of the patient.

13) THE THERAPIST USES TEACHING AS A TOOL TO SUPPORT EMOTIONAL GROWTH.

Being aware of values and beliefs helps therapists to maintain honesty with themselves, and encourages openness and clarity with clients. The assumption that it is desirable to be aware of our beliefs puts therapists in a position to know what they are teaching clients.

Part of what therapists do is teach what they know about life experience to clients, even though their way is not the only way to think about things. By being aware of his or her beliefs, the therapist can support the client in coming to his or her own conclusions, even when they differ from that of the therapist.

In this way, the client is protected from the unconscious "selling" of values by the therapist as a result of his or her countertransference.

An example of clarifying beliefs in therapy is found in a verbatim therapy session by Michael Basch in *Doing Psychotherapy.* On pp. 152 and 153 he responds to a patient who has already told of a dream in which a man treats him affectionately. In that context, he had also expressed his somewhat nostalgic wish to have a woman be sexually interested in him. Basch continues:

"Therapist: The basic theme that I detect in your story is that of being shown that you are wanted and desirable. In your dream you were being kissed by the man, in your phantasy (sic) you are being undressed by a woman who has let you know she wants you. You recall that in real life the only girl you became close with, Nancy, approached you in the library and let you know that she liked you.

"My guess would be that the being kissed and held and tenderly undressed were things that your mother did, perhaps in those years when you had her all to yourself before you father came home. These memories remain permanently fixed in some form as a source of comfort to which you return, disguising them to suit the occasion, when the present seems not to offer warmth and receptivity.

"Holding, hugging, and kissing. These are some of the ways in which a child is shown that he is worthwhile, a precious being. From that comes a healthy self-love--identity, self-esteem, self-respect --call it what you will. If we're not satisfied that we truly are worthwhile, we can spend the rest of our lives looking for that affirmation in whatever we do. It's a hidden agenda that is operative in all our behavior, unbeknownst to us. A need that must be fulfilled before we can go on to reach other emotional goals.

"So I think we can hazard an answer to your question about your sexuality. It's not a matter of homosexuality versus heterosexuality, but a matter of priorities. There's something you have to get done first before you can fulfill adult needs. You must settle for yourself the issue of whether you are a worthwhile, desirable person. You will look at whomever you're with, regardless of gender, and in whatever situation you find yourself, for an answer to that. And because it is an issue from many years ago you'll want it answered in the way you would have needed it then. Will they hug me, hold me, touch me, and kiss me, or at least let me know by how they look at me that I am precious to them? Or will they abandon me to my own devices to cope as best I can, literally and figuratively, untouched in my loneliness?

"George: [*Laughs]* Sorry, I'm not laughing at what you said.

"Therapist: I know, everything fits doesn't it? From infancy on when what was disorganized or confusing falls into place and lets itself be understood, we laugh with pleasure."

The sessions went on with George continuing to make progress, using his self-understanding to take charge of his own life and relationships. The teaching of the therapist helped George experience his past in a new way. The therapist believed in the liberating power of understanding old beliefs in a new way.

14) THE THERAPIST USES POSITIVE ACTION AS A WAY TO CONFRONT SELF-DEFEATING BEHAVIOR.

The belief that symptoms are solutions provides a positive basis for the therapist to understand and plan what to do with a client. Solution-oriented therapy is one way of emphasizing this point, that we can change what we do in order to get better results in everyday living. By focusing on our goals, we can identify faulty ways of achieving them and deal with our own resistances to doing what will be effective.

Even before solution oriented therapy became popular, symptoms were understood to be ways of dealing with emotional stress. Dr. Herbert Holt, an existential therapist, tells of an initial meeting with a patient in his book, *Free to be Good or Bad,* which was published in 1976.

He describes a woman who had married as a kind of exchange: she would do all the wifely things, and her husband would look after her so that in her old age she would not have to worry about taking care of herself. She did her part for twenty five years, so that when she came for her consultation with Dr. Holt, she was in her forties, but in a wheelchair, pushed by her husband, looking haggard and old.

She had been to many doctors, who ruled out organic problems, and was considering surgery to relieve her chronic, debilitating back pain. Her coming to see Dr. Holt was a last-ditch effort to relieve her pain before resorting to surgery. He describes the encounter as follows:

> "They were barely inside the door when her husband blurted out, 'This is the last —after this I am through! I have taken her to doctor after

doctor, but she is too sick, I have no more patience with this. I wouldn't watch a dog suffer like this.'

"His overbearing, bullying tone offended me and I said, mildly enough, 'But she is not a dog, she is your wife.' When he answered in the same offensive way I said, half-joking, 'You're are a sourpuss! To live with a man like you could give anyone a pain!'

"I glanced at the woman and saw that she had raised her head — she was actually listening. So I took a chance and went on to deliver a lecture on human compassion and empathy for another's suffering. I said, 'It would not surprise me to discover that you are your wife's pain. It just might be that your attitude toward her is the cause of your wife's affliction.'

"'Yes!' his wife suddenly exclaimed. 'Yes, yes, yes!' She was sitting forward in her wheelchair and her face had come to life. So I continued, expanding on the theme of how one person can cripple another one, emotionally and even physically, by treating the other as a function, a mechanical convenience, never as a human being.

"I did not say that, of course, the other also contributes by submissively accepting this treatment — she was not ready for that. Her husband spluttered but I did not let him speak. She was nodding at my every word, offering now and then a confirming comment of her own. About half an hour went by, and then her voice suddenly rang out.

"'Doctor, I have no pain!' she cried. 'For the first time in seven months I have no pain!'

> "That was only the beginning of her cure; an illness that had developed over twenty-odd years could not be dissipated in twenty-odd minutes (pp. 153-154)."

Holt goes on to describe the onset of her pain, when during an argument her husband threatened to find a nice young wife, and then dump her. She suppressed her urge to kick him in the groin, and that night had a dream in which she lost her leg. In the dream, her mother said, "I told you to be careful. . . ." and she awoke terrorized but could not sit up because of the sharp pain in her left leg. The pain eventually was so debilitating that she was limited to a wheelchair as a means to move about, up to the time of this therapy session.

This example is of an unorthodox beginning of therapy by an existential analyst, illustrating an application of the assumption that symptoms are solutions, long before the concept became familiar to the public.

He confronted her self-defeating ways of solving her emotional conflicts, and the way her husband contributed to the endless vicious circle in which she lived. While he did not use an "ordinary" therapeutic technique, he gave her the modeling and permission to use other options than her paralysis to achieve some of the relief she was seeking. She responded by giving up her paralysis as well as her massive emotional dependence on her husband.

Holt's belief that her symptoms were the equivalent of a faulty solution to her own internal emotional conflicts and external interpersonal conflicts with her husband formed part of the basis and power of his successful treatment of her.

15) THE THERAPIST LISTENS TO THE WISDOM OF THE CLIENT, KNOWING THE THERAPIST'S WAY IS NOT THE ONLY WAY.

No theory or technique is ultimate. When this is an operational assumption of the therapist, he or she will be interested in listening to the wisdom of the client, knowing that the therapist's way is not the only way to success.

Perhaps the most common application of this principle is for the therapist to focus on what is emotionally most important to the client.

Richard Chessick gives an example of this focusing by choosing what to respond to in a dream. In *How Psychotherapy Heals,* pp. 59 and 60, he quotes a dream fragment presented by his female patient:

> "I am at a dinner party seated between my sister-in-law and my mother-in-law. I feel quite trapped. Mother-in-law is a good cook, but sister-in-law is taking the credit for her cooking. It is a nasty situation."

Chessick adds the following comments about the dream:

> "One might make a mental note of the oral and homosexual elements in this dream, as well as the defensive mechanisms of denial and displacement. This fits previous formulations about the patient. In terms of dealing with the patient, however, I chose the feeling of being 'trapped' to discuss. It was the predominant feeling in the dream, and led to a tremendous

> release of feelings about her husband and the marriage. . . .
>
> "The principle followed here was to try to relate the dream material to the focus of therapy at the time of the dream, and to deal with the dream in terms of the material of the therapy, even though this means neglecting important deeper elements for some future date."

A therapist operates within the frame of reference of his or her theory system, in this case psychoanalytic. Whatever the therapist's theoretical frame of reference, he or she can be guided in the therapeutic work by the client's wisdom, which includes knowledge about what is emotionally important, and what is needed to deal with the important issues.

The therapist in this case stayed within the client's focus, waiting for a sign from her at a later time to deal with the "deeper" elements, even though that might have seemed more "significant" to him. Such selectivity is inevitable, since everything cannot be focused upon at once. Faith in the timing wisdom of the client was integrated here with the perspective of the therapist as he formulated what to say and do to make the therapeutic process most effective.

CONCLUDING REMARKS

Fred Kuether, our training director at the American Foundation of Religion and Psychiatry in 1962, leaned back in his chair, inhaling as he put his feet up on the desk. He had been asked by one of the residents in pastoral psychotherapy, "What is the most important thing to do with a patient?" We were just beginning our three year residency, and were eager to learn from this "master."

He spoke slowly and deliberately, as was his habit, to give emphasis and importance to his words. "Listen," he said, "and understand what is being communicated."

Listen, and Understand

Listen, and understand. It seemed a bit mysterious, at the time. But we did understand that he meant to take the client seriously, pay attention, and attempt to see things from within the client's frame of reference. We did not, at the time, understand that if we did what he suggested, we would also be taking a position of spiritual attentiveness.

By listening, we would communicate the implicit message that "You are important, because you are there. I will endeavor to see the logic of your point of view and let you know I understand it's validity for you. Furthermore, I will look for what it is in your point of view that I see as being valid from my point of view as well. I will look for ways I can empathize with your emotional pain and joy, even though we remain separate persons knowing that my feelings are not the same as yours."

These are some of the values we learned from Fred, who expressed them in the way he treated us as well as the way he treated clients and others. He offered us much I did not fully understand.

Faith in Values

As therapists and as human beings, we all believe in values on which we base our lives. Those values have a hierarchy of importance, in that some are so fundamental as to be identified with who we are. Other values are less basic, and may be up for re-evaluation and some modification from time to time.

We live by faith in our values and by faith in whatever other realities we find meaningful in our lives, whatever name we give them. Some persons who have a significant religious history may speak of their highest reality with the name of God. Other therapists would not do so, but have their own alternative way of symbolizing what they consider to be most high and most real.

We endeavor to speak the language of our religious or non-religious clients, in order to communicate most clearly, and with some may never speak of God. For other clients, speaking in religious terms may be a clearer way to communicate and touch the truth in a healing way. But however we do it, we communicate our faith to our clients, though we seldom call it that. We endorse values we consider to be most high and most real, though we don't usually speak to our clients directly of our values.

We Communicate Our Faith Stance

We model the commitment to what is most important in our own lives by the way we *treat* our clients, friends, and families. As much as we may sometimes wish to be not so transparent to others, we are transparent anyway, since our thoughts, feelings, and behavior illustrate our values and our faith.

Whatever else is true, we are who we are at any given moment. The inevitability of our being ourselves, as we are, just now, underlies the most significant value assumption of all. That assumption is not only that we exist, but that we have value simply because we exist, and that others have value in the same way.

This is an affirmation of life for ourselves, for others, and for all creation. This loving attitude connects us to a dimension of life in ourselves some call spiritual, and is the avenue for our personal, emotional participation in all reality.

While beyond words and definition, being ourselves is our opportunity to participate in the evolution of life from birth through old age. Being ourselves is our opportunity to create the experience of being who we are, of choosing for ourselves, and of charting our course in life in our own way.

Being ourselves is our opportunity to participate in the small world in which we grow up, the larger world we explore, and the universe we are part of before exploring even begins. Being ourselves as we were genetically designed to be can be understood as cooperation with God, a participation in his Spirit, a fulfillment of our humanity.

Our values reflect our experience of being who we are, our experience of the world as it is, and the ways we put the two together. As therapists and human beings, we pass along our values, whatever else we do, and hope that what we have to offer can be used to enrich the lives of others, as well as our own.

INDEX

REFERENCES

Andrews, Sperry, (1996). "Promoting a Sense of Connectedness Among Individuals by Scientifically Demonstrating the Existence of a Planetary Consciousness." *Alternative Therapies,* 2(3), 39-45.

Basch, Michael Franz, (1980). *Doing Psychotherapy.* New York: Basic Books.

Basch, Michael Franz, (1988). *Understanding Psychotherapy.* New York: Basic Books.

Buber, Martin, (1953). *I and Thou.* New York: Charles Scribner's Sons.

Chance, Jeremy, (1999). *Principles of the Alexander Technique.* London: Harper Collins Publishers.

Chessick, Richard D., (1969). *How Psychotherapy Heals.* New York: Science House.

Clinebell, Howard, (1992). *Well Being.* New York: Harper Collins.

Dossey, Larry, (1993). *Healing Words.* San Francisco: HarperSanfrancisco.

Dossey, Larry, (1996). "What's Love Got to Do With It?" *Alternative Therapies,* 2(3),4-7.

Erickson, Milton H., (1983). *Healing in Hypnosis, Vol. I.* New York: Irvington Publishers.

Erickson, Milton H., (1985). *Life Reframing in Hypnosis.* New York: Irvington Publishers.

Erikson, Erik H., (1964). *Insight and Responsibility.* NY: W. W. Norton.

Fagan, Joen, and Shepherd, Irma Lee, eds., (1977). *Gestalt Therapy Now.* New York: Harper & Row.

Ferré, Nels, (1947). *Faith and Reason.* New York: Harper.

Fowler, James, W., (1980). *Becoming Adult, Becoming Christian.* San Francisco: Harper and Row.

Fowler, James W., and Browning, Don S., eds., (1987). *Faith Development and Pastoral Care.* Philadelphia: Fortress Press.

Frost, S. E., Jr., (1958). *Ideas of the Great Philosophers.* New York: Barnes & Noble.

Gardner, Richard A., (1971). *Therapeutic Communication with Children.* New York: Science House, Inc.

Glasser, William, (1975). *Reality Therapy.* New York: Harper & Row.

Goulding, R. L., and Goulding, Mary M., (1978). *The Power is in the Patient.* San Francisco: TA Press.

Hawking, Stephen, (1988). *A Brief History of Time.* New York: Bantam Books.

Hayakawa, S. I., (1964). *Language in Thought and Action.* New York: Harcourt, Brace, & World, Inc.

Hersen, Michel, Kazdin, Alan E., and Bellack, Alan S., eds., (1983). *The Clinical Psychology Handbook.* New York: Pergamon Press.

Holt, Herbert, (1976). *Free to be Good or Bad.* New York: M. Evans and Company.

Hunter, Rodney J., ed., (1990). *Dictionary of Pastoral Care and Counseling.* Nashville: Abingdon Press.

James, Muriel, ed., (1977). *Techniques in Transactional Analysis.* Reading, Mass:, Addison-Wesley.

Kutash, Irwin L., and Wolf, Alexander, eds., (1986). *Psychotherapist's Casebook.* San Francisco: Jossey-Bass.

Lewis, Helen Block, (1971). *Shame and Guilt in Neurosis.* New York: International Universities Press.

Moyers, Bill D., and Flowers, Betty Sue (Ed.), (1993). *Healing and the Mind.* New York: Doubleday.

Napier, Augustus Y., with Whitaker, Carl A., (1978). *The Family Crucible.* New York: Harper & Row.

Philips, J. B., (1958). *The New Testament in Modem English.* New York: The Macmillan Company.

Rogers, C. R., (1957). The necessary and sufficient conditions of therapeutic personality change. *Journal of Consulting Psychology, 21,* 95-103.

Rossi, E. L., (1986). *The Psychobiology of Mind-Body Healing.* New York: W. W. Norton.

Shapiro, Francine, (1995). *Eye Movement Desensitization and Reprocessing: Basic Principles, Protocols, and Procedures.* New York: Guilford Press.

Sifneos, Peter, E., (1992). *Short Term Anxiety-Provoking Psychotherapy.* New York: Basic Books.

Stokes, Kenneth, ed., (1983). *Faith Development in the Adult Life Cycle.* Minneapolis: Adult Faith Resources.

Stricker, George, and Gold, Jerold R., eds., (1993). *Comprehensive Handbook of Psychotherapy Integration.* New York: Plenum Press.

Tillich, Paul, (1948). *The Shaking of the Foundations.* New York: Charles Scribner's Sons.

Ulanov, Ann and Barry, (1975). *Religion and the Unconscious.* Philadelphia: The Westminster Press.

Von Glaserfeld, (1984). *The Invented Reality.* New York: W. W. Norton.

Westerman, Michael, "A Hermeneutic Approach to Integration: Psychotherapy within the Circle of Practical Activity," (1993). *Comprehensive Handbook of Psychotherapy Integration.* New York: Plenum Press.

Whitaker, Carl A. and Bumberry, William M., (1988). *Dancing with the Family.* New York: Brunner/Mazel.

Wolberg, Lewis R., (1988). *The Technique of Psychotherapy.* Philadelphia: Grune & Stratton.

Yapko, Michael D., (1988). *When Living Hurts.* New York: Brunner/ Mazel.

Yapko, Michael D., (1992). *Hypnosis and the Treatment of Depression.* New York: Brunner/Mazel.

Zeig, Jeffrey K., (1987). *The Evolution of Psychotherapy.* New York: Brunner/Mazel.

Zeig, Jeffrey K., and Munion, W. Michael, eds. (1990). *What is Psychotherapy?* San Francisco: Jossey-Bass.

BENJAMIN B. CONLEY, M. Div., LMFT

A practicing psychotherapist, Benjamin B. Conley is an ordained Elder in the United Methodist Church, a Diplomate with the American Association of Pastoral Counselors, a Clinical Member of the American Association of Marriage and Family Therapists, a certified Imago Relationship Therapist, and a level II EMDR therapist.

Licensed in Florida as a Marriage and Family Therapist, he has had additional training in TA/Gestalt therapy, hypnotherapy, sex therapy, with extensive experience teaching and supervising individual and group psychotherapists, marriage and family therapists, clergy, and other mental health professionals.

After completing his three year clinical residency at the Blanton-Peale Graduate Institute in New York City in 1965, he co-founded the Foundation for Religion and Mental Health in metropolitan New York in 1968, providing community counseling services and clinical training for clergy and mental health professionals.

He also served for three years as director of an inservice training program for medical and clerical staff at the Memorial Sloan Kettering Cancer Institute in New York City, and has served as Training Director of the Samaritan Counseling Centers of South Florida and as an adjunct faculty member in the Doctor of Ministry Pastoral Counseling program at Garrett Evangelical Theological Seminary in Evanston, Illinois.

In 1987 he moved to Fort Lauderdale, Florida, with his wife, Rena, who practices as a licensed psychologist, and son, Ryan, to join the staff of the Samaritan Counseling Centers of South Florida.

Order Form

The Spiritual Connection: Values, Faith and Psychotherapy ISBN: 0-9708221-4-6 (256 pp. softcover) is available in the following quantities and prices:

				Shipping:
1 to 2 copies	$ 29.95	Each	plus	$ 4.50 total
3 to 5 copies	$ 25.95	Each	plus	$ 2.00 per book
6 or more copies	$ 20.95	Each	plus	$ 1.50 per book

Postal orders: Send check and order filled in below to:
Anthos Publishing, P.O Box 4304B, Ft. Lauderdale, FL 33338-4304
Credit card purchases may be made at:
www.anthospublishing.com or 1-(800) 247-6553

Sales tax: Please add 6% for books shipped to Florida addresses.
Shipping: Use rates above. Shipping will be by priority mail.

Please send the following books. I understand that I may return any books in new condition for a full refund -- no questions asked.

I enclose $___________(including shipping and tax, if applicable)

for _____copies of The Spiritual Connection and

for_____ copies of______________________________

Name: ____

Address: ______________________________________

City:__________________________ State:______Zip:________

Email:____

Visit: www.anthospublishing.com **Email:** orders@anthospublishing.com

OTHER AVAILABLE BOOKS BY BENJAMIN B. CONLEY

Making Relationships Work	-	1995	48 pages softcover	$6.99	- $2.00 Shipping
Affirming Feelings	--	1994	60 pages softcover	$7.99	USPS book rate
The Meaning of Love	--	1993	52 pages softcover	$6.99	for each book
Success in Marriage	--	1998	48 pages softcover	$6.99	listed here.